Chapter 1

A Christmas Party

Sidney Sinclair stared gone at the falling snow. The flakes fluttered down gently, some fast, some sluggish. All of them thawing immediately upon contact with the damp ground.
She sighed and pressed her face versus the freezing glass. "Stick!" she shouted. She waited eagerly for snow every wintertime, however snow hardly ever lingered in Tennessee. It was usually as well warm. Sometimes, like now, the small flakes barely even touched the ground before going away. She viewed with any luck, wishing with all her might that the ground would certainly ice up so the snow would certainly begin to accumulate. She would certainly be disappointed if she didn't a minimum of obtain enough snow out of this little storm to make a snowman.
" Sidney," her mother called from the cooking area. "It's virtually time to go. Are you all packed up?"
" What do you assume?" she yelled back with a smile, jumping up from her seat by the home window. She had actually packed her overnight bag hours before and also had everything she would certainly need for Mrs. Fitzpatrick's pajama party in a cool pile by the front door.
Mrs. Fitzpatrick was the owner of Blue Moon Stables, a riding secure simply across the roadway from Sidney's residence, as well as she had actually decided to have a sleepover event to commemorate the holidays. Her riding pupils, Sidney included, had been looking forward to it for weeks, but Mrs. Fitzpatrick refused to speak about the specifics of the party. She desired every little thing to be a shock, that made the pupils a lot more distressed for the big day to arrive hand.

Her mommy showed up in the living room door, a covered plate in

Sidney inhaled deeply. "Gingerbread?" she guessed.
Her mother nodded as well as grinned, her green eyes dancing. "Made.

particularly for you.".
Sidney licked her lips and held out her hands to take the plate, but Mrs.

Sinclair realized the tray tightly, holding it just out of her reach. "Not yet, Sid. We have to save some for the other party-goers.".

" I'll just lug it," Sidney pleaded, tilting her head to seek out at her mommy as innocently as she could. Her mommy tightened her eyes, however offered home plate to Sidney. The glass bottom really felt warm against Sidney's hands.

" Mmm. Just out of the oven?".

" Yes, ma'am. And also I much better not capture you creeping a bite." Mrs. Sinclair winked at Sidney as well as ordered her silly eco-friendly Christmas sweatshirt off the rear of the sofa.

" Don't fret," Sidney responded. "You will not capture me ..." Sidney shook a finger as well as giggled under the light weight aluminum foil covering the gingerbread. While her mom pulled the candy-cane-covered coat over her head, mussing her ginger-colored hair, Sidney snapped off a little piece and popped it right into her mouth. She attempted to keep back the groan of satisfaction.

" I hear biting," her mother stated, glancing in the mirror by the front door. She corrected her hair and also combed the wrinkles out of the sweatshirt with her hands. "How do I look?" She twirled for Sidney like a ballerina. Sidney swallowed her bite of gingerbread and also licked the crumbs from her lips.

" Beautiful," Sidney claimed. As well as she meant it. Mrs. Sinclair always looked stunning to Sidney, and she wanted to look much like her when she matured. They currently looked a great deal alike, and also Sidney's mommy in some cases called Sidney "mini-me". The only large distinction in between the two was their eyes.

Sidney's mom had shimmering green eyes, while Sidney had brown eyes, the same as her dad.

" Let's go, after that, Sid. I'm ready to consume some scrumptious holiday food. I hear Mrs. Fitzpatrick makes some killer hot delicious chocolate," her mommy claimed as she opened up the front door, allowing a blast of chilly air. Sidney shuddered and stepped out right into the wintry weather.

" Brrr. It's cold out here. Let's rush, Sid." Mrs. Sinclair banged the front door behind them and locked it quickly then strode off towards the roadway. Sidney tried to run ahead of her mother, yet simply breathing the icy air made her lungs hurt. Reducing her actions, she stuck her tongue out, stretching it as for it would certainly go to try to capture a few snows on her tongue. The fragile snow didn't taste in all, however she suched as to really feel the flakes

thaw and disappear in her mouth.
Mrs. Sinclair, who had Sidney's bags in tow, didn't discover Sidney lagging behind, so Sidney took the opportunity to creep another bite of gingerbread.
" I desire Dad was right here," Sidney said regretfully, chewing on her bite of stolen cookie. Gingerbread reminded her of him. Her mommy really did not like gingerbread, however her dad did, and also it was something they constantly shared throughout the vacations. He was the best at structure gingerbread residences, as well as he always let Sidney embellish his masterpieces.
" He would certainly be if he could, Sid. He'll be back this evening, though."
"Just not in time for the party?".
" Just not in time for the party," her mommy duplicated.
" He's never ever been out of town this near to Christmas before.".
Mrs. Sinclair really did not respond. She just pursed her lips and also proceeded strolling.
Mr. Sinclair's work took him out of town commonly, but he usually reserved the week before Christmas as well as the week after just for family time. In the beginning, Sidney hadn't thought him when he stated he 'd be leaving for a day or more, which he 'd miss Mrs. Fitzpatrick's Christmas celebration. It just had not been like him. But he'll be back this evening, Sidney thought, as well as I'll see him initial thing when I get residence tomorrow morning. We'll make our gingerbread residences with each other.
That's what he had actually assured Sidney before he left.
" I'm thankful the stables are so close to house," Mrs. Sinclair claimed. "This snow just could begin to stick nevertheless. It's cold out right here.".
The flakes hurt Sidney's face as well as her bare hands, and the cold made her nose red as well as numb.
" I need to've put my handwear covers on," Sidney said to her mom. Holding on to the plate of gingerbread with icy fingers, she quickened her actions to capture up, and her mother glanced back, a concerned look on her face.
Mrs. Fitzpatrick had actually told the riding trainees to bring their riding gear, but Sidney had actually chosen to simply put on hers rather. She had worn her warm winter months coat over an old flannel tee shirt and a used pair of jeans. She had finished the set with a beat-up set of utilized cowboy boots she had picked up at the neighborhood tack store. Her mom had opposed against her attire, yet Sidney had insisted. She felt comfy in her riding equipment which's what she intended to use. Besides, she had actually spiced it up a bit, linking her red hair back with a green ribbon to include some Christmas joy.
" Where are your gloves?" Her mommy frowned. "In my bag. Don't fret. I

really did not forget them." Mrs. Sinclair sighed. "You much better not have.".

Sidney understood her mommy didn't wish to return house to search for them. Sidney's handwear covers never ever seemed to stay in a set. She was commonly sent out to the barn using mismatching gloves because real match couldn't be found. She had actually currently shed 2 sets of handwear covers completely and winter months had hardly started. Her sock situation had not been far better, but a minimum of if she needed to wear one blue sock and also one red one, her boots covered it up.
Sidney avoided past her mom and towards the large, brightened barn.
"Almost there! Hurry up, Mom!".
A couple of vehicles were parked in the barn whole lot, and also Sidney could listen to voices within.
Sidney began to go toward the big barn doors, which caused the barn. aisle and also the stalls, but her mommy quit her.
" Not this way, Sid," she claimed promptly. "You understand the celebration's being kept in the brand-new addition.".
Mrs. Fitzpatrick called the new enhancement to the barn her "Christmas existing to herself". It would certainly be used for sleepovers as well as celebrations. The addition featured tables for crafting as well as games, two small spaces with bunk beds for sleeping, a small kitchen area, two bathrooms with several stalls and also a shower an item, as well as a small classroom total with a whiteboard as well as desks. Sidney had actually walked through the brand-new enhancement often times while it was in building and construction, however Mrs. Fitzpatrick had actually been maintaining the area off limits while the final touches were included. This would certainly be the very first time Sidney would certainly see it completed.
" I just intended to greet to Jasper and the others.".
Her mom gestured toward the white door that resulted in the brand-new addition. "Not now, Sid. Let's enter into the event.".
Sidney furrowed her eyebrows. Mrs. Sinclair had an unusual view her face, as well as she really did not meet Sidney's questioning gaze.
" Don't you believe it's even more courteous to say hello to the people first rather than the steeds?" her mother proceeded, going down Sidney's garments bag so she could wipe snow from the shoulder of her coat.
She didn't wait on Sidney to address. Marching as much as the door, she knocked carefully in between the branches of a huge irritable wreath. Sidney

and also Bryan, Mrs. Fitzpatrick's boy, had enhanced the wreath together only a few days previously. Sidney had put mini plastic horses all over the border, and Bryan had wrapped a red bow around the wreath, linking a large, pretty bow at the top.

The door opened as well as Mrs. Fitzpatrick beamed at her guests. "Come in, Sidney. Come in, Cara. I'm so grateful you might make it. We've had several students phone call to state they weren't coming because of the snow. Although it doesn't appear to be sticking.".

Mrs. Sinclair wheezed with relief as she stepped into the warmth of the barn addition.

" And bad Kelsey," Mrs. Fitzpatrick continued, "she was meant to be below, but she traveled out of state to see family members, and obviously it's a great deal worse there. The snow is accumulating, and also she couldn't get a flight back.".

" Kelsey will not be below?" Sidney frowned, dissatisfied. Kelsey was a junior riding teacher at Blue Moon Stables, and she had been Sidney's camp counselor at Camp Sycamore Streams. She was a wonderful cyclist and a good friend. Sidney had actually been expecting seeing her. Kelsey had not been offering as numerous lessons at Blue Moon Stables since college started. She would certainly be relating to universities soon and also being a senior in secondary school was maintaining her busy.

" Well, we're lucky in that regard," Mrs. Sinclair responded, "because we live simply nearby. No problem for us to obtain right here.".

" Yes, you and the Abbots," Mrs. Fitzpatrick stated, gesturing for them to come in from the cold.

Sidney ordered the bag her mommy had actually dropped outside the door as well as followed her into the entranceway. "Speaking of the Abbots, is Jane here yet?" Sidney peered around the room as she peeled off her coat and also hung it on a fix by the door.

" Not yet, I'm worried." Mrs. Fitzpatrick frowned as well as pursed her lips. She trembled her head and also her brown ponytail whipped to and fro. "Seems she's been delayed. Her mother called and also stated they should be right here soon, though.".

Mrs. Abbot, Jane's mommy, lived next door to Sidney and also her family, as well as the Sinclairs recognized the Abbots well.

" That's unusual. She's never ever late to anything. Specifically when it entails Christmas," Mrs. Sinclair stated, concern in her eco-friendly eyes. "She's always the initial to get to these kind of things.".

Mrs. Abbot commemorated the vacations like she did whatever else: completely and seriously. She tossed events, enhanced extensively, and also handed out presents to every person. It was Christmastime if there was one time of year Sidney appreciated and suched as Mrs. Abbot.

" Well ... I would not fret. She'll be below quickly enough." Sidney's riding instructor offered Mrs. Sinclair an appearance that Sidney comprehended. An appearance that said, "I'll inform you later", as well as Mrs. Sinclair responded and allowed the issue decrease.

" We were almost to dig in," Mrs. Fitzpatrick continued, blazing a trail right into the large, open location where the crafting tables had actually been established.

Trays as well as plates brimming with food and also beverages were shown on every surface, both in the craft location and in the adjacent cooking area. Sausage rounds, chips and also dip, cookies, fruit, fancy sandwiches ... Sidney's eyes expanded vast as she looked at all the goodies.

Mrs. Fitzpatrick eliminated her of home plate filled with gingerbread, packing it in between a white cake decorated with environment-friendly and also red sprays as well as a tray full of brownies.

" Are those your overnight clothes?" Mrs. Fitzpatrick gestured towards the bag Mrs. Sinclair still held.

" No, these are Sidney's books as well as video games.".

The riding trainer had recommended the students to bring along video games they assumed would be fun to play in a team, as well as Sidney had actually brought along some publications. She had entered the practice of analysis during the night prior to she went to sleep, as well as she hesitated she would not have the ability to drop off without a book in her hands.

" My clothing remain in the bag I left by the door," Sidney stated. "Why do not you take your clothing right into bunkroom 2?" Mrs.

Fitzpatrick fidgeted with the Christmas-themed fabric on the table, pulling it in this manner which, careful not to knock off any kind of food, until the edges were also. "I'll put the games with the others and I'll introduce your mom to various other students and also their family members. Every person else is in the class. I put a Christmas motion picture on the television therein, yet it's almost over.".

Sidney went and nodded to get her carry-on from the entrance. She transported it into the 2nd bunkroom, which was simply off the kitchen area, as well as discarded it on the local bed. The thick canvas felt a bit damp due to the melting snow, so she wiped her hands on her denims and also, on 2nd

idea, picked the bag up and dropped it next to the bed. She really did not desire the sheets to splash, and also besides, she would need to wait on Jane to pick bunks. They always bunked together.
As she was standing there assuming as well as wondering when her close friend would arrive, she heard something. Murmuring. Coming from the kitchen area.

Peering around the entrance, Sidney held her breath. Her mother and Mrs. Fitzpatrick had currently returned from doing away with the other bag as well as had their heads together in the cooking area. They were speaking softly to one another while they discovered the food.
" ... she's ready ... regarding time ... liable ... I hope ...".
Sidney really did not pay much interest to what they were stating up until she heard her name. She simply found it intriguing that her mother and Mrs. Fitzpatrick were murmuring to each other and presumed it concerned Mrs. Abbot not being there on time.
" Sidney ... matured so much ... I'm afraid ...".
Sidney tightened her eyes at both. What were they saying about her? Sidney stressed to make out their words, however she could only capture snippets of the conversation. The majority of it was drowned out by the sound of crinkling foil and also plastic as the covers were eliminated from all the trays as well as plates.
" ... shock ... anxious ...".
That sounded like her mother. Sidney peered around the entrance. Part of her felt guilty about listening in, yet a larger part of her desired to get closer and also hear more. It seemed like a secret, as well as a juicy one. And also it included her, so why shouldn't she recognize?
She saw Mrs. Fitzpatrick shake her head while she leaned over the bowl of punch on the cooking area counter. "Definitely not ..." The riding teacher laid out paper cups by the bowl and put a huge dipper into the red liquid. "She needs it ...".
Mrs. Sinclair started to react to whatever Mrs. Fitzpatrick had actually claimed, however she gazed towards the bunkroom and saw Sidney watching.
She broke her mouth closed as well as pasted on a fake smile. "Sidney! Why do not you go tell everyone it's time to eat?".
Mrs. Fitzpatrick whirled around to stare at Sidney, also, her hazel eyes wide. She swiftly recouped as well as complied with Mrs. Sinclair's lead with an uplifting smile. "Yep! Time to consume! You can be our messenger.".

Sidney just stared. She couldn't think it. She had actually been caught eavesdropping, and her mother as well as Mrs. Fitzpatrick were the ones who seemed ashamed and also embarrassed.

They're definitely hiding something.

" Go on, Sid." Her mommy kept her eyes on home plate she was eliminating from the microwave. "This food will get cold again.".

" What were you talking about?" Sidney asked, enjoying them suspiciously. Both females avoided her look.

" Nothing, Sid," Mrs. Sinclair stated, as well as she fluttered her hands at her child as if to shoo her away. "Go.".

Sidney put a hair and grinned of hair behind her ear, trying to reduce her excitement. She enjoyed a great mystery, and also this was certainly mysterious. She had never ever seen her mommy act so peculiar.

" Of program," she stated, "I'll be right back." And also she avoided off to make the statement prior to her mom had time to realize she should be in trouble.

Chapter 2

Party Games

After eating up until they could stuff themselves say goodbye to, the partygoers' moms and dads started to trickle out right into the cold. They would certainly be back in the early morning to get their children, however several of the kids didn't seem to recognize that. For several of the youngsters, this was their very first sleepover, and a few of the more youthful children got teary-eyed. Mrs. Fitzpatrick stepped in with games as well as diversions in those cases, and the mother and fathers offered peace of minds, hugs, and kisses, as well as headed out into the snow, which had begun falling greatly.

Mrs. Sinclair was the last to leave. Before she left, she curved down and provided Sidney a quick peck on the cheek, murmuring "I like you" in her ear. Sidney was depressing to see her go. Not since she had actually never ever been to a sleepover before, yet because she hadn't had a chance to identify what her mommy had actually been talking about with Mrs. Fitzpatrick yet, as well as she had not also considered an excellent way to begin her examination right into the issue. Just how would she ever fix the enigma if her mother was gone?

Mrs. Sinclair unlocked and peered outside.

" It's getting cooler around at all times!" she said loudly. She crossed her arms over her breast as well as glimpsed back at Sidney. "I believe I also see a few flakes in the turf. We could have some snow on the ground in the early morning.".

Bryan came to look past Mrs. Sinclair, his eyes broad. "Do you truly assume so?".

" I wish so, for your sake. See you tomorrow, Sid." Mrs. Sinclair chuckled as well as provided one last wave prior to heading out into the thickly falling snow. Bryan took her place at the door, getting to a distribute to capture a few flakes.

" Can we turn on the information, Mom, as well as see what they're saying?" Bryan shouted back to Mrs. Fitzpatrick.

" If you closed that door you can," Mrs. Fitzpatrick shivered and also gestured towards the class where the TV was established, still running Christmas motion pictures. "Don't let the cool air maintain leaking in here.".

Bryan raced and knocked the door off toward the class with Jimmy, a fellow riding student as well as another buddy of Sidney's. Sidney had.

met both Jimmy as well as Bryan when she had started taking lessons at Blue Moon Stables the previous year. They had actually all taken courses together, and they had all invested the summer together at Camp Sycamore Streams, too. Tonight, Jimmy had actually brought along his little sibling for the pajama party. Jared had actually recently started taking lessons at Blue Moon Stables, and also he suched as to comply with Jimmy around almost everywhere he went. He admired his older sibling, and replicated him in both motion as well as outfit. Jimmy had actually worn his typical jeans as well as a plaid, buttoned-down t shirt with old, beat-up cowboy boots to the event. Jared's outfit looked much the same, and he swaggered behind the two older boys right into the class.

" Is Jane still coming, Mrs. Fitzpatrick?" Sidney was starting to fret. It was 5 o'clock and also really nearly dark outside. Every person had currently eaten and the games were about to begin. Jane was missing out.

" As much as I know," the riding instructor replied. Pulling at her brown braid in frustration, she frowned and also glimpsed up at the clock. "She ought to be right here anytime now. In the meanwhile, we may need to begin without her.".

Then, the door ruptured open again, as well as Sidney's buddy, Jane Abbot, was available in with a flurry of snow. Her cheeks were rosy with cool and also her nose was as red as Rudolph's.

She tore off her mittens, wheezing.

" There you are, Jane." Mrs. Fitzpatrick sighed. "I was beginning to ask yourself.".

" Everything's all set," Jane claimed with a smile. Mrs. Fitzpatrick responded, a happy expression on her face. Jane ran over to hug Sidney, her blue eyes dance.

" What's all set?" Sidney asked. It appeared like every person at the party had something up his/her sleeve.

Jane put a finger to her lips as well as ordered Sidney's hand, dragging her aside. "Mrs. Fitzpatrick has a surprise.".

" Is that where you've been?".

Jane responded, her short blonde hair appearing and also down. "My mom's been aiding organize it, and I selected her.".

Sidney pressed Jane's chilly hand. "Can you tell me?".

Jane opened her mouth to spill the beans but never ever obtained the opportunity. Mrs. Fitzpatrick clinked her glass of eggnog with a fork as well as all eyes turned toward her.

" Listen up, my young riders. It's time for the video games to start

Abandon the board games for the moment. Leave them just as they are and we'll complete them after the parlor game!"

" Party games?" the riding trainees whispered amongst themselves. A few of the more youthful youngsters neglected her as well as proceeded having fun, however the older children cheered up.

" There will certainly be rewards awarded for the champion of every game. And I have the utmost reward for the victor of one of the most video games." Mrs. Fitzpatrick held out a golden horseshoe. The letters CPGC had been repainted throughout the top. "The winner of one of the most games will certainly be crowned the Christmas Party Games Champion as well as he or she will certainly get this horseshoe in addition to a present card to Barney's Tack Shop."

" A genuine prize?" Jimmy cried out. He stood and also crossed his arms. Bryan had sidled back in from the classroom as well as stood alongside Sidney. He and Sidney exchanged glances. Jimmy was affordable, especially when it involved video games, as well as he had a quick temper. He never ever backed down from an obstacle, which Sidney admired, however he did get rather disturbed when he lost.

Jimmy's little bro, who sat on the flooring close by, smiled up at him. "You'll win for sure, Jimmy."

" Don't be so certain, Jared." Jimmy glared around in all the various other children. "Looks like we've got some intense competition." When he claimed it, he smiled, however Sidney recognized he was really evaluating his rivals, and she rolled her eyes.

" What would certainly they say concerning the snow?" Sidney murmured. Bryan's brown eyes beamed. "It's beginning to stick. They said an inch, possibly two, by early morning."

Jane ordered Sidney's arm and enriched and also down. "Snow! We can build a snowma, and we can go sledding, as well as have a snowball fight!"

Bryan grinned at Jane, getting to across Sidney to give her a one-armed hug. "I'm pleased you made it. Mother was stressed you wouldn't. Is it all set?" Mrs. Fitzpatrick fired a dark look in their instructions and they dropped quiet. However as soon as she averted, Jane nodded excitedly.

Mrs. Fitzpatrick continued holding the horseshoe up for every one of them to see, and a few children also got up from their seats to obtain a more detailed look at it. "So, are you ready to compete for this?"

Mary, a brand-new student at the stables, sneered at the honor. "I wouldn't mind the gift card. I can use it to buy Sadie a new halter, yet that horseshoe's second best. It's just a routine old horseshoe with gold paint and also letters on

it."
Mrs. Fitzpatrick claimed not to hear her, as well as Sidney felt her blood start to steam. Mary had actually only been riding at Blue Moon Stables for a few weeks. When Sidney initially satisfied Bryan, she got a poor first impression, but he turned out to be a terrific friend, so when Mary occurred, she battled difficult to offer Mary a possibility, but the new woman appeared figured out to wreck everybody's fun regularly. She continuously criticized the various other cyclists and also their equines, and regularly bragged about all the ribbons she had won with her gorgeous Quarter Horse, Sadie, at neighborhood shows.
Sadie was an expensive show horse and also absolutely nothing like the lesson horses at Blue Moon Stables. Sidney really did not assume that made her more important or extra unique than the other equines at the barn, but Mary sure appeared to think so. Sadie boarded at Blue Moon Stables, and Mary and her dad, Mr.Wright, had given Mrs. Fitzpatrick specific instructions for her treatment, consisting of a note that asked no one else to touch her. So, Sidney and Bryan, that both worked in the stables, were asked not to handle Sadie, and Mrs. Fitzpatrick needed to look after Sadie all on her own.
" I assume it's special." Jimmy tightened his blue eyes at Mary, his shoulders stooped ahead angrily. He would certainly had much more difficulty with Mary than the rest of them. He couldn't aid however react to her disrespectful remarks, and it commonly got him right into problem with Mrs. Fitzpatrick, who appeared reluctant to scold Mary.
Mary shrugged her small shoulders and reduced her eyes, pulling back from the group bordering Mrs. Fitzpatrick.
" Anyway," the riding trainer claimed, offering Jimmy a refusing look, "we should start now. The very first video game will be pin-the-tail-on- Jasper!"
Jane got Sidney's hand and also drew her forward to get in line. A blown up photo of Sidney's favored lesson equine, Jasper, held on the wall behind one of the craft tables. Mrs. Fitzpatrick handed the initial pupil in line a phony horsetail with a tack connected to it as well as a blindfold. "Let the video games begin!"

***

Somehow, Mary ended up winning not simply the initial game, but the 2nd. As well as the 3rd game, music chairs, didn't end well for the

various other students either.

" Cheater!" When Mary slipped previous him as well as right into the last chair, Jimmy called out. There was no way he might reach the chair without knocking her down.
" She didn't rip off, Jimmy," Mrs. Fitzpatrick said sternly. "That isn't very great. She reached the chair first."
" You were just too sluggish." Mary stuck out her tongue at Jimmy behind Mrs. Fitzpatrick's back, but the riding instructor turned just in time to see it.
" That's not wonderful either, Mary," Mrs. Fitzpatrick stated. "I won't have that habits from either of you."
Mary shrugged and also crossed her arms while Mrs. Fitzpatrick obtained the prize for the music chairs video game, a tiny glass porcelain figurine of an equine and cyclist, and offered it to Mary.
" That's stunning," Jane gushed, running over to obtain a closer look. The delicate glass equine had its front unguis raised and also its head thrown back with its mane blowing in the wind. The biker looked off right into the distance with one hand securing his eyes from the sunlight. "They appear like travelers."
Mary grasped it close to her upper body, away from Jane's gaze. "Can we play the next game now?"
Mrs. Fitzpatrick sighed, glimpsing about at the disgruntled trainees. Mary winning 3 video games in a row had not reviewed well. "Let's take a quick break while I do the evening feedings in the barn. Everyone can get a drink and also a snack and after that we'll end up the games. How does that sound?"
Jimmy whined, brushing a hand via his unpleasant blond hair. "I believe we must simply obtain it over with. It's obviously rigged." He muttered as he stomped off toward the refrigerator.
Bryan provided Sidney a short lived look of frustration and followed close behind him. "I'll support him up," he promised as he passed Mrs. Fitzpatrick.
" And I'll aid you feed the steeds," Sidney piped up.
Mrs. Fitzpatrick trembled her head. "Not this evening, Sidney. I desire you to appreciate the celebration, and that suggests you are definitely restricted to be in the barn. Remain in right here and enjoy with your pals. I'll be back in a couple of minutes and we can obtain the games going again."
Sidney started to say, but Mrs. Fitzpatrick provided her an appearance that Sidney understood implied business, so she closed her mouth as well as relied on Jane rather.
" Let's pick bunks. I was awaiting you."

She hadn't had a chance to tell her about the bits of conversation she had actually overheard in between her mom as well as Mrs. Fitzpatrick, and also she intended to do so in private.

***

" It has to have to do with a Christmas present, best?" Jane claimed quietly, storing Sidney's bags under the bunk they had actually selected to share. "I heard my mama telling my daddy that she acquired me a brand-new sweater and new riding boots for Christmas simply last week. I didn't intend to destroy it, so I acted like I didn't listen to anything. I'll need to pretend to be surprised when I open them."

" New riding boots?" Sidney plunked as well as giggled down on the bed. "You simply obtained a new set a few months earlier. Does your mom think you need brand-new boots each time you obtain manure or mud on them?"

Jane rolled her blue eyes skyward and also frowned. "Pretty much. You know Mom. Back to your problem ...".

" What do you think it is? And also why would she be fretted about it?" Sidney frowned. "I simply can't consider anything to discuss it, and also it's scaring me.".

Jane tapped her finger on her chin. "I do not understand. It is strange, Sid, but you'll learn quickly sufficient if it's something to do with Christmas. It's only a week away.".

" Maybe-" Sidney began, however she never ever got to complete her thought. Mary ruptured right into the space, rips streaming down her face.

" Sidney?" Mary sniffled as she combed wisps of raven-colored hair from her wet cheeks. "Mrs. Fitzpatrick says she needs you.".

Sidney stood up swiftly from the bunk. "What's incorrect?".

Mary took a deep, rattling breath. "It's Sadie. I assume she's ill.".

Chapter 3
Sadie's Bellyache

Sidney as well as Jane followed Mary from the bunkroom as well as back right into the event area. The other kids appeared unfazed. Several of them chomped on treats as well as drunk from plastic mugs, while others sat on the floor or at the craft tables finishing the board games they had actually abandoned when the parlor game began.

Mary sobbed gently while she led the women throughout the space as well as to the door that divided the brand-new enhancement from the real barn. She glimpsed back as her hand touched the handle. "No one else is intended to go in," she claimed to Jane. "Some type of shock.".

Jane reached out and also placed a reassuring hand on the girl's arm. "I understand about the shock, however I'll wait right here and also make certain no else bothers you.".

Mary shrugged Jane's hand away and also nodded, splits still spilling from her troubled eco-friendly eyes. She had a hard time between emotions, appearing mad, unfortunate, as well as thankful all at the same time.

" Let's go," Sidney said, giving Mary a nudge. She didn't want her to damage down in front of every person. It would certainly be humiliating for her as well as upsetting for everyone else. Sidney's heart rate enhanced as the two girls slipped via the door quietly, leaving Jane to stand guard inside.

The door opened up into a little barn workplace Mrs. Fitzpatrick had actually fashioned from among the stalls. The new wooden floors gleamed, but the beat-up wooden workdesk in the corner was currently used and well-used. Sidney understood that was where Mrs. Fitzpatrick kept all her documents on the equines. As soon as over, she offered the space a quick. A brand-new phone had actually been set up. It hadn't been there the last time Sidney had actually remained in the office. It was on the desk in the middle of a selection of papers and documents that looked like they were waiting to be sorted as well as submitted.

" Through here," Mary said, leading the way through the workplace door and right into barn aisle.

The freezing air struck Sidney, taking her breath away, as well as she shuddered. She had grabbed her coat, however it just wasn't thick sufficient to stay out the cold.

The barn doors were closed, but she might still really feel a wind from somewhere.
The wind must be picking up available.
" And there's the shock." Sidney stopped short appropriate outside the office door. "How did they obtain that point in here without any individual seeing?".
A large red sleigh occupied much of the barn aisle. It had actually been embellished for Christmas with glossy brass bells as well as brightly colored tinsel. Like Santa's sleigh. There was something various concerning this sleigh. Rather than the snow runners frequently seen on sleighs, this had wheels so maybe made use of also when there wasn't any kind of snow. Sidney recognized it had not been really Santa's sleigh, yet she couldn't take her eyes off of it. It looked magical in some way in the dark light of the barn.
Mary hardly glanced at it before hurrying off towards Sadie's delay. She stopped impatiently to touch her foot on the ground and also gesture for Sidney to comply with when she recognized she wasn't behind her.
" Come on," she hissed, tossing her head. "Mrs. Fitzpatrick's waiting.".
Sidney tore her stare far from the sleigh, as well as ran down the barn aisle towards Mary unwillingly. She normally suched as the nighttime noises of the stables, however tonight the serene audio of the equines tearing hay from their mangers and eating contentedly had actually been replaced with troubled movements and also frustration. Jasper, the huge black gelding she usually rode throughout lessons, stuck his head over the top of his stall door as she passed as well as bumped her arm with his nose. She quit long enough to pat the horse affectionately, and also he whinnied gently, his nostrils fluttering underneath her gloved hand.
" It's alright, kid," she whispered. "It's nothing to bother with.".
Mary reached Sadie's stall as well as peered over the stall door, a worried view her face. Sidney listened to a groan from inside.
Mary moved for her to hurry, as well as Mrs. Fitzpatrick's emerged over the delay door as she popped up from where she must have been kneeling. "Oh, good, Sidney," she stated. "I require your aid.".
" What do you desire me to do, Mrs. Fitzpatrick?".
" I need to stay with Sadie. I've called the Wright's veterinarian, but he doesn't understand when he'll be able to get here. He's got various other situations and also the snow is really slowing things down. I need a person to hop on the phone with all the vets in the area. This is an emergency. We require a veterinarian here today. Call every veterinarian close by.".
" But, Mrs. Fitzpatrick, Dr. Teller is the very best. That's why my daddy selected him as Sadie's vet." Mary squeezed the delay door so difficult her knuckles.

turned white. The splits still streamed down her face, yet she really did not seem to observe.
" I know that, Mary, yet Dr. Teller might not be able to make it in time. We need a person here immediately, and he's on the opposite of community, in the snow, with an additional person.".
" But ..." Mary's voice trailed off and she viewed the verge of collapse. Sidney had actually never ever seen any individual so upset. She got hold of Mary by the hand. She could feel how cool the girl's skin was also with her gloves. "Come on, Mary. Help me in the office. You can seek out the veterinarians' numbers for me while I call them.".
Mrs. Fitzpatrick nodded gratefully, however she still looked concerned. "By the means, Sidney, have you seen Bryan as well as Jimmy?".
Sidney drank her head. "Bryan stated he was going to support Jimmy up. That's the last time I saw them. Possibly they headed out in the snow.".
Mrs. Fitzpatrick shrugged and gave a frustrated sigh. "I might truly use his help right now. Exists somebody accountable keeping an eye on the youngsters? I suggested for him to do it.".
" Jane's in there, Mrs. Fitzpatrick. She will not allow the more youthful ones do anything dangerous.".
" Good." Mrs. Fitzpatrick reversed to her cost.
Sidney glimpsed the horse for the very first time, and what she saw made her tummy clench. Sadie was down on the floor of her stall. Wood shavings hold on to the steed's upper body and also sides, sticking to her sweat covered body. The generally patient, silent equine seemed sweating a lot in spite of the freezing temperatures, as well as she had a hurt search in her eyes.
Sidney turned Mary far from the scene and also led her back to the workplace. She pressed the workplace door closed behind them, shutting out the cold, as well as removed her coat. She handed it Mary. "Wipe those tears away prior to they ice up on your face. We need to reach function. Sit here," Sidney took out the workdesk chair, "and also check out this for regional vets. Beginning making a list of the closest ones." Sidney rifled through the drawers up until she found a phonebook and plopped it down on the desk before the woman.
" And I'll use this emergency listing. Give thanks to benefits Mrs. Fitzpatrick is always prepared." A list of emergency numbers was taped to the desk next to the phone, as well as Sidney dipped into it swiftly. Three veterinarians were provided in addition to the get in touch with details for a farrier as well as a couple of emergency situation numbers in instance of a fire or a student injury.

Dr. Teller was the given name on the contact sheet, however Sidney

understood he had actually already been called, so she skipped his name as well as went on to the next one.
Mary enjoyed her face very closely as she called the first veterinarian. Sidney discussed the scenario to the individual on the other end of the phone, paid attention for a moment, then shook her head. Mary looked back down at the telephone directory, crestfallen. The following phone call was the same. It was an active, and also awful, evening. The climate had not been on their side.
Sidney sighed. "Next number.".
" This isn't functioning." Mary scrunched up her face, which was currently inflamed from sobbing, to try to keep the flow of splits at bay. "No one's going to come.".
" Someone's going to come." Sidney clinched her teeth together. "Give me a number from the telephone directory.".
Mary rattled off a number. "His office gets on the opposite side of town.".
Sidney dialed as quick as she could. She paid attention to the rings while she scrubed Mary's shoulder reassuringly.
" Dr. Parson's workplace.".
Sidney took a deep breath and launched into a description of their trouble for the third time. The woman on the various other end of the line listened politely, asking inquiries when ideal.
" We need somewhere here now," Sidney stated ultimately. "It's actually. poor.".
" I comprehend. Dr. Parsons is out on a phone call today. Let me provide him. a ring on his cell as well as I'll call you right back, sweetheart." "Okay," Sidney claimed. "Thank you a lot.".
" Just a minute." The line went dead, and Sidney established the phone down. "She's going to obtain in touch with him. He's out on a phone call.".
The door to the brand-new enhancement opened up as well as Jane stuck her head in. She looked shocked to see them resting at the workdesk. "What's taking place?" she said, attempting to keep her voice reduced.
Sidney upgraded her as rapidly as she could, all the while looking at the phone, willing it to ring.
Jane responded curtly when she completed. "I'll keep an eye on the children. You simply obtain a vet to Sadie.".
Jane drew the door closed to get back to the younger kids.
Brrrng. Brrrng.
Sidney had the phone approximately her ear in a jiffy, prior to the second ring.

had even ended up.
" Is he coming?" she spouted out.

The woman on the other end chuckled gently. "You're in luck. He just finished up with one more person and he happens to be nearby. I gave him the address. He ought to be there in concerning 10 mins.".
Sidney's heart rose and she patted Mary on the back smiling widely.

" Thank you!" she said loudly to the female. "And Merry Christmas!" "Merry Christmas to you, too," the woman replied. "I wish every little thing.

turns out all right.".
Sidney hung up the phone and also skipped off to tell Mrs. Fitzpatrick fortunately. She went outside to wait on the vet. Mary chose her.
She couldn't bear to stick with Mrs. Fitzpatrick and also Sadie, and also Sidney really did not think it was an excellent suggestion for her to remain with them anyway. Her anxiousness just made matters worse.
For the very first time, Sidney felt a little bit uneasy with lady. They had actually never been alone prior to or had a real conversation. Mary's snippy mindset had actually transformed Sidney off from the get go, so it had actually been difficult to even carry on small talk at the barn.
" You appear truly close to Sadie," Sidney stated to load the quiet. The snow had actually certainly started to stick, as well as huge, fat snows fell heavily from the sky. It seemed to stifle out all the sound. "How long have you had her?".
Mary sniffled and also rubbed her nose. "A long period of time." She thought twice as well as glanced sidewards at Sidney. "My mother offered her to me.".
" Really? I've never ever met her. Your father constantly brings you to lessons,. right?".
Mary's jaw clenched. "Yes. You won't be fulfilling her. She died.
when I was 8.".
Sidney nearly wheezed, yet she held it in. "Oh, I'm so sorry. I had no suggestion.".
Mary shrugged and averted however Sidney really did not see any type of splits. She's possibly used them all up. "I usually don't bring it up. Individuals act unusual when they understand.".
It held true. Sidney really did not know what to claim. Simply envisioning shedding her very own mom brought tears to her eyes as well as made her feeling numb around. And also, she felt humiliated that she hadn't known. She ought to have been more sensitive.

Sidney put an arm around Mary's shoulder. This time around, the girl made no move to shrug it off or avert like she had from Jane.
" I'm certain Sadie will certainly be fine."
" I wish so," Mary claimed. "She was the last present Mom offered me, and also the most effective. She offered her to me for my 8th birthday celebration. Daddy really did not want to get me an equine, however Mom insisted. She stated I was worthy of one after working so hard."
This details splashed out of her quickly, like she had actually been holding it in for a very long time. "I've had her for 3 years now."
They dropped silent, viewing the snow. "I believe it's going to be greater than an inch or two," Sidney said. She cleaned snow from her shoulders as well as drank her head to obtain it out of her hair. A fine dusting had currently covered Mary's ebony hair, and snow hold on to her unclear green coat around, making it show up stippled in color.
" You're really efficient the video games. Exactly how do you keep winning?"
"Just good luck, I think." Mary offered Sidney a small smile.
" Well, simply wait until this summertime. Mrs. Fitzpatrick told me she is going to include horseback games to the lessons. Type of such the games they play in a gymkhana. You would certainly be amazing at that."
Mary responded enthusiastically. "They made use of to have those competitions at my old barn. Timed video games on horseback and races and stuff. They were a great deal of enjoyable." She stopped briefly as well as scrubed her nose once again. It had actually turned brilliant red in the cold. "Sadie always liked contending."
" Well, you ought to speak with Mrs. Fitzpatrick about it." Sidney tried to keep her tone light. "Maybe she would certainly also have a show right here at Blue Moon Stables."
" That's a great suggestion. There's the vet, I believe." Mary aimed. Two beams of light shone with the snow as well as lit up the road before Blue Moon Stables, exposing a thin sheet of white on the black asphalt. The roads are getting negative. It's a good idea he was so close.
The motorist turned carefully right into the driveway as well as killed the engine, walking up the hill on foot.
" Easier simply to park down there, I believe," he claimed when he rose to the barn, a bag full of medicines and also veterinary tools on his arm. He wore thick coveralls and also heavy boots covered with mud, and he had a sandy-tinted beard that almost looked white with snow. He looked cold and exhausted, but he smiled kindly at both ladies. Sidney discharged a breath and also grinned back.

His presence was reassuring.

" The client's this way," Sidney stated. She led the veterinarian right into the barn, grateful to have her component of the task finished. Mary complied with close behind both. "Would you such as a drink or anything?" Sidney asked as a second thought. The male looked virtually iced up. And also he'll most likely be out in this weather for a while. Sadie's most likely not his last person of the evening.

" That would be nice. If you've got anything warm."

" Mrs. Fitzpatrick makes the best hot chocolate." Sidney smiled at the older guy. "I'll put in added marshmallows."

He grinned and pulled his hat down reduced over his ears. "Perfect. It's nippy out tonight. Why don't you ladies obtain all of us a cup and I'll look after this horse. What's the individual's name?"

Mary took a deep breath, as well as grabbed Sidney's hand. "Sadie. Her name's Sadie."

Chapter 4

Stolen

Prizes

When Sidney as well as Mary came back the celebration, turmoil had actually followed. Jane still stood protecting the door, her blue eyes vast.

" What's taking place?" Sidney asked as one of the more youthful kids, a kid she had never ever seen prior to, raced past her, hardly staying clear of a crash. An additional little kid, that appeared to have actually been chasing after the initial, slid to a stop right in front of Sidney and smiled at her, his face smeared with white icing and also chocolate. "Tag! You're it!" he screamed and also slapped a sticky hand right into her belly prior to removing again.

" Oof!" Sidney leaned over.

" I believe he desires you to chase him, Sid." Jane giggled. The wild little young boy stopped about ten feet away and danced instantly, sticking his tongue out at Sidney.

Sidney massaged the spot where the child had slapped her as well as made a face right back at him. "This is precisely why I do not help with the younger youngsters' lessons. They're crazy."

" I believe they're just obtaining agitated. And they're eating too many sweets." Jane gestured at the massacred treat table. "Don't fret. I haven't let them do anything hazardous. How's Sadie?"

" Well, the veterinarian's right here. So, ideally, she'll be fine. Mrs. Fitzpatrick has to remain out there as well as help him. We was available in to obtain some warm chocolate."

" I'll assist you make it."

Mary excused herself to the washroom to clean up her tear-swollen face while the various other ladies mosted likely to the kitchen area to warm up some water.

Sidney had actually just poured the steaming water right into two mugs filled with Mrs. Fitzpatrick's special hot delicious chocolate mix when she listened to a scream. She set the frying pan down swiftly, her hands trembling, and whirled about. But prior to she might state anything, Jane took fee.

" What is going on?" Jane demanded, in as intimidating a voice as she could. Jane had not been a very harmful sort of person, so it took a great deal of initiative for her to appear this way. "Who yelled?"

Every person iced up. For the first time, the celebration dropped entirely silent. All the various other riding students looked at Jane, stunned.
" I'm significant," Jane continued. "I need to know that screamed right this second."
A little woman with lengthy blonde braids stood up her hand reluctantly. Her lower lip shivered.
" It was you?" Jane claimed in a kinder voice.
The girl trembled her head and also directed. At Jared, Jimmy's little brother. Jared's face went light, however he didn't reject it.
" Why did you do that, Jared? You terrified us."
" I can not discover my brother. Derek said he left me right here." Jared directed at the kid resting next to him, a brief, mean little kid whom Sidney had the bad luck of knowing rather well. He went to riding lessons two times a week, as well as his mommy occasionally left him at the barn for hrs after his lesson instead of selecting him up right away. Sidney felt sorry for the child. She understood he disliked being left at the barn, but he could be a genuine discomfort. He liked to play tricks on her if she took place to be at the stables as well as would follow her around making fun of her as well as laughing at whatever she did. Derek held his hands up in the air innocently. "Well, he did, really did not he? He's not below."
Jane glanced at Sidney, as well as Sidney drank her head. She had no concept where Jimmy had gotten to.
" Your sibling didn't leave you, Jared," Jane guaranteed him. "I do not know where he is, yet he's right here someplace. Is Bryan. They simply went off somewhere together. Come below with us." She held up a hand as well as Jared trotted over. "We'll make you a mug of warm delicious chocolate."
Jared smiled unwillingly as well as understood Jane's fingers.
" I recognize why they ran off!" Derek claimed unexpectedly, a malicious smile on his face. He indicated the place on the table where Mrs. Fitzpatrick had stacked the prizes for the parlor game. "The horseshoe is gone. Is the gift card.
The rewards have been taken!"
This time Sidney stopped the outcry. She quieted the muttering group with an upraised hand, assuming Derek was just trying to cause difficulty, however when she looked at the table, she saw he was right. The horseshoe as well as the envelope including the gift card had actually been gotten rid of from the table.
" This isn't funny. Where are the rewards?" Sidney crossed her arms as well as

blazed at the gathered kids consequently, but nobody answered.

***

Sidney handed Mrs. Fitzpatrick a cozy mug of steaming cacao as well as patted her arm. She looked exhausted. Slight creases had started to reveal around her brown eyes, and also her mouth drooped uncharacteristically. Her brownish ponytail even appeared limp.
" Well, things didn't go as prepared tonight, did they?" she stated with a. laugh.
Sidney smiled sadly and also drank her head. "I'm sorry, Mrs. Fitzpatrick. I understand you spent a lot of time planning this celebration.".
" We can constantly have an additional celebration. I just wish Sadie will certainly be okay.".
Sidney concurred silently. She could not forget what Mary had told her out in the snow. Sadie was a special horse, as well as she implied a lot to Mary. Sidney saw as the youngsters raided the kitchen. She had actually upgraded Mrs. Fitzpatrick on the situation with the missing prizes, as well as Mrs. Fitzpatrick had actually been let down to say the least. She had sent out Jane off searching for Bryan and also Jimmy, and she would certainly had the children tidy up the mess they had actually constructed from the location as well as search for the missing horseshoe as well as present card at the same time.
" No luck," Mary claimed, cleaning a strand of black hair from her eyes. She had relaxed after the veterinarian got here and ceased her crying, however the tenseness in her shoulders and the terseness of her voice offered her fear away. Sadie had not been out of the timbers yet, and Mary would not fully relax until she understood her horse was safe.
Mrs. Fitzpatrick drank her head. "It really was simply a horseshoe, Mary. Like you claimed. Do not bother with it.".
" Oh, but I really did not indicate it, Mrs. Fitzpatrick. You recognize that.".
The riding instructor put an arm around Mary's shoulders. "I called your daddy regarding Sadie.".
Mary sought out hopefully. "Is he coming?".
" He claimed he would certainly wait up until early morning. The snow is simply excessive tonight.
It's even worse than everybody assumed it would certainly be.".
" I assume we're going to get a whole lot," Mary agreed.
The front door banged open as well as snow whirled in, the flakes blowing

about the area on a blast of freezing air. Jane ran in, embracing herself to keep warm, as well as Bryan and also Jimmy followed her. Neither would fulfill Mrs.Fitzpatrick's eye.

" Sorry, Mom," Bryan said. "We didn't recognize any individual was trying to find us.".

" We'll discuss that later, Bryan," she responded sternly. "Right currently. we need your aid looking for our missing out on prizes. Did Jane tell you?".

Bryan nodded as well as snow showered from his shaggy brownish hair onto the flooring, swiftly thawing to form tiny puddles around his sneakers.

Jimmy blazed at Mary. "Maybe she took it.".

Mary rolled her eyes. "Why would I take it? I was already going to win it anyway.".

Sidney snorted, attempting to hold in her laughter, and also Jimmy transformed his mad gaze on her.

" Be great, Jimmy," she claimed. She was made use of to his temper and affordable spirit, yet she understood he was a huge softie at heart. "Did you find out about Sadie?".

Jimmy shrugged and also looked away. "Yeah. I'm sorry concerning your equine, Mary. I wish she'll be fine.".

An awkward silence chosen the team, and also Mrs. Fitzpatrick grinned. "We can get along, people. We all have something alike. Our equines. And also most of us love Blue Moon Stables, right? You all like your riding trainer?" She winked and also grinned at Jimmy.

" We do most of the time," he responded with a teasing smile. Everyone grinned.

" We all like Christmas, and the snow," the riding trainer proceeded. "And most of us intend to enjoy tonight, do not we?".

The trainees nodded.

" Good. Can you help me to make that happen?" The team nodded once more.

" Then let's forget the rewards in the meantime. I can constantly obtain another reward. It does not have to be provided this evening." She gripped her hands in front of her as well as beamed. "Let's go Christmas caroling!".

" Can we take the sleigh like we planned?" Jane asked.

" What sleigh?" Jimmy's eyes obtained broad, but Mrs. Fitzpatrick shook her head.

" I'm scared not. The roadways are obtaining too bad. It's on wheels, bear in mind, because we really did not understand it would in fact snow. We'll have to do it the antique method.".

" Sleighs are pretty antique." Jimmy placed his hands on his hips. "Nobody uses them any longer.".

" Well, a lot more old-fashioned. We're going to be walking. Assist me organize the kids. I have candles for us to bring. And also we can go sing Christmas carols.".

" At my house?" Sidney asked excitedly. "And Jane's?" Mrs. Fitzpatrick responded. "And the remainder of the area.".

***.

" We're dreadful at this, but I do not also care," Jimmy claimed as they shuffled from Jane's front yard to the Sinclairs' front backyard. Sidney could see the Christmas tree she and also her mother had set up weeks before beaming in the porch window. With the snow swirling before the comfortable little residence and also the smoke seeping out of the smokeshaft, it looked like a photo from a Christmas card. As Sidney admired the pretty scene, her father's face showed up in the leading pane of the home window.

" Hey, Dad," Sidney called, waving for him to come out. He gave her a big smile and also disappeared. The front door opened a minute later on as well as both of Sidney's parents appeared onto the patio, covering themselves up in their layers.

" He made it back from his trip sound as well as safe," Sidney said to Jane with fulfillment.

Mr. Sinclair put an arm around Mrs. Sinclair's waist. He looked happy as well as ecstatic, as well as both eyed each various other and also smiled secretively. Something's up and he learns about it, as well. Sidney narrowed her eyes at her parents as well as shouldered Jane, however before she might articulate her thoughts to her best friend, Mrs. Fitzpatrick took her place in front of the group and swung a riding crop like a conductor's adhere to obtain their interest. "Ready? Silent Night!".

The carolers introduced into the song, some starting prematurely, some too late, as well as a lot of them off key, however it seemed magical to Sidney. She promptly neglected her bother with her parent's surprise, as well as offered her complete energy to the tune.

At one point, she glanced over at Jimmy. He had his hand on Jared's shoulder, and also Jared sought out at him with beaming eyes.

When the team stopped briefly for a breath in between songs, Sidney aimed the wonderful scene bent on Jane. "Jared just venerates him," Sidney said. "Isn't it adorable?".

Jane realized Sidney's gloved hand and also provided it a press. "He's charming. I.

wish Jimmy dream pay more attention to focus. He attempts very tough to excite him.".

Sidney concurred quietly. Jimmy had not been always sensitive to other individuals's feelings, and also he appeared entirely unaware of his brother's appreciation.

" I would supply you hot delicious chocolate," Sidney's mommy phoned call to the carolers, "however after having Mrs. Fitzpatrick's, it would certainly taste terrible, and also I'm sure this team has actually had plenty of sugary foods already.".

" You have no idea," Mrs. Fitzpatrick claimed noisally, trembling her head. She had actually cheered up considerably considering that they had actually begun caroling. She and Mary had left their problems at the barn with Dr. Parsons. At first, Mary had demanded sticking with her horse, however the vet had actually guaranteed Mary he 'd be with Sadie until they returned, which wouldn't be long.

The carolers chuckled as well as, led by Mrs. Fitzpatrick, continued on their way. Sidney's parents offered her a final wave and also enjoyed as she followed the group towards the following home, about a fifty percent a mile down the road.

" Caroling was an excellent idea," Mr. Sinclair claimed, seeing the youngsters track off. "They're going to be exhausted by the time they return after traipsing with the snow. They'll possibly drop right into bed.".

Mrs. Sinclair giggled as well as placed an arm around her spouse's shoulder. "Do you think Sidney's guessed? She heard something, but I could not tell just how much.".

He drank his head. "She would've said something if she recognized. You know exactly how she is. I assume she'll be excellent and shocked.".

Mrs. Sinclair shivered, extra from enjoyment than the cold. "I can't wait. This is the most excited I've been for Christmas in a long period of time.".

" I know what you mean." Sidney's daddy looked up at the snow. The flakes danced happily in the soft glow of the veranda light. "There's something various regarding this year. It seems like there's a little magic in the air.".

The pair retreated right into the warmth of the Sinclair house, and the Christmas carolers treked off to spread their Christmas cheer, none of them aware that simply throughout the road, up in the barn, something enchanting was undoubtedly occurring at that very moment.

Chapter 5

A

Discovery

Sidney tumbled down onto the bunk and also snuggled into the Western-design comforter, wrapping the blanket comfortably around her icy feet.
" Oh, it feels like paradise." Sidney groaned, shaking her thawing toes.
A warm, comfortable glow cleaned over her, and her eyes felt all of a sudden heavy.
Jane climbed the little ladder to the top bunk. The bed squealed as she tunnelled under the covers over Sidney's head. "Night, Sid," she murmured.
" Night, Jane," Sidney whispered back.
Sidney's dad had been. The lengthy go through the chilly as well as snow had actually exhausted the team. Sidney can already listen to a carolers of snores around her and also the lights hadn't even been turned out yet.
Mary was the only one who really did not look tired. She simply looked miserable. When the group had actually made it back to the barn, the vet had actually refused to allow her see Sadie. He even had the nerve to smile at her when she whined. "Just a few even more minutes," he had claimed, as well as he had giggled.
" How could he laugh?" Mary claimed to Sidney. It was the fourth or 5th time she had claimed it.
Sidney sighed. Mary had picked the bunk right across from she and also Jane's, as well as rather than lying down to go to sleep like every person else, she sat with her knees prepared to her chin. It appeared like the rips will begin once more so Sidney edged out from under her warm covers reluctantly and went to sit beside her.
" I'm certain it's since he recognizes she'll be great," Sidney claimed.
Jane peered over the top of the bunk. "You must simply go to sleep, Mary. When you get up, she'll be much better.".
Sidney picked and nodded up Mary's cushion to compel it right into her hands. "Sleep. Keeping up all evening won't help anything. Besides, Mrs. Fitzpatrick guaranteed to find obtain you, whether you're sleeping or not, once the veterinarian leaves.".
Mary approved the pillow, yet her eyes weren't on Sidney, they were on the area where her cushion had been. "Where did those originated from?" Mary claimed, her voice trembling. "I really did not place them there.".

Sidney reversed, and also she gazed, too. A glossy golden horseshoe, the missing out on reward, as well as the gift card stocked the area where Mary's pillow had actually been.
" Someone hid them under my cushion," Mary said, puzzled. Sidney didn't state anything. She was just starting to like Mary.
Could she believe her? Why would any individual conceal the rewards under her cushion?
Jane climbed below her bunk. She tried to hide the rewards once again prior to anyone can see, however among the other women had already identified them.
" She took the rewards!" The lady screamed, aiming at Mary. "They discovered them. It was her! We should go tell Mrs. Fitzpatrick.".
Jane attempted to shush the girl, yet she wasn't having it. She jumped from her bed as well as raced away to get Mrs. Fitzpatrick. Another woman complied with and the rest looked up sleepily from their bunks. Some interested, some upset.
Mary aimed to Sidney and also Jane frantically. "You think me, do not you? I really did not take them.".
Sidney was reluctant, however Jane concerned the girl's protection. "Of course our team believe you, Mary. Why would certainly you want to steal them? You would certainly've won them anyhow.".
Sidney had to admit Jane was. Mary had currently won numerous prizes that night, and also she most likely would have won these rewards. "And you were with us a lot of the moment," Sidney included.
" But who would do this?" Mary wept out, taking the horseshoe from Jane. "Why would somebody wish to mount me?".
Jane shrugged and combed her mussed hair back from her face. "I don't recognize.".
Sidney understood, however, and she knew Jane did, also. She was just as well good to claim it. Mary wasn't preferred, as well as her snippy attitude had actually transformed a lot of the riding pupils against her. Several of them would certainly enjoy to see her in trouble.
" I believe it's simply a mean trick," Sidney said. "Someone wants to get to you.".
Mary stopped as well as ran her finger over the side of the glossy metal footwear. "Because I was suggest to them?".
Sidney as well as Jane considered each other helplessly. Prior to they were compelled to respond, Mrs. Fitzpatrick came in, complied with by the two women that had actually run off to obtain her.

"What's taking place?" the riding teacher said. "You located the video game prizes?"
Mary held the horseshoe out, and Jane handed over the present card. Mrs. Fitzpatrick took the rewards with a smile. "Thank benefits, ladies.
I'm so delighted."
" But she took them, Mrs. Fitzpatrick," the angry lady behind Mrs. Fitzpatrick argued, her hands on her hips. "She should be punished, should not she?"
Mrs. Fitzpatrick took a look at Mary seriously. "Did you take these, Mary?"
Mary shook her head, her eyes solemn. "No, ma'am. I have no concept just how they arrived."
" That's great sufficient for me." Mrs. Fitzpatrick shrugged her shoulders. "There's no harm done. We have them back now."
" But isn't she mosting likely to be penalized?" The lady that had tattled asked, searching for at Mrs. Fitzpatrick with broad eyes.
" No, Penny. Whoever took them shouldn't have, yet it is Christmas, isn't it? A time for forgiveness?"
Dime moaned and also stomped away, flopping onto her bed with gone across arms. Sidney sighed with relief. Mrs. Fitzpatrick had leapt to conclusions regarding her in the past, equally as Sidney had about Bryan when they had actually very first met, as well as she had hesitated that Mrs. Fitzpatrick would certainly assume the most awful regarding Mary. They had all discovered some tough lessons since then, though. Mrs.
Fitzpatrick winked at Sidney as if reading her thoughts. "Besides, I've assumed regret in the past, and I was incorrect. Can you prove that Mary took the rewards?" Mrs. Fitzpatrick asked Penny. "She says she really did not, as well as I think her."
Cent shook her head, her brown braids flying, and blazed at Mary, who looked away shyly.
" If anybody else had taken it, they would certainly have been penalized. You simply allow her get away with anything because her mom's dead."
Everybody gaped at the woman as well as Mrs. Fitzpatrick gasped audibly. "How attempt you, Penny? What a dreadful thing to say. That's not real in the least."
Mary shook her head. She considered the horseshoe in Mrs. Fitzpatrick's hand after that stared right back at the lady. "No, it holds true, Mrs. Fitzpatrick. I've been bad-tempered as well as mean, and also you've allow me bemean since you were as well great to hurt my feelings."

" Mary-" Mrs. Fitzpatrick started.
" No, let me ask forgiveness. I won't be bad-tempered as well as mean any longer. I didn't take those." Mary gestured towards the rewards. "But my actions has been undesirable. And also my mommy never ever would have allow me act that way." Mary paused and gazed right at her accuser. "I'm sorry, Penny."
Penny seemed to unwind a bit. The sneer gradually went down from her face, and she hung her head. There was a long minute of silence, after that Penny spoke, her voice shivering. "I should not have actually raised your mother. I'm the one that ought to be sorry."
" No, I should not have dealt with every person so severely. Do you assume you can forgive me? I assure to stop being such a Negative Nancy."
Cent snorted and gave Mary a tiny smile as well as a curt nod.
Mrs. Fitzpatrick looked in between the women and trembled her head. "You girls are growing up, resolving your problems.You don't also require me, do you?"
Mary reached out and also took Mrs. Fitzpatrick's hand. "I do. Can I go see Sadie now?"
Mrs. Fitzpatrick bent down and also covered her arms around Mary, providing her a fast capture, then she pulled her up from the cushion. "Yes, you can. In fact, I was almost to come get you anyhow. I have a shock for you."
" I don't understand if I can deal with anymore shocks," Mary said. "Can Sidney as well as Jane come, too?"
Sidney searched for at her riding instructor with pleading eyes.
" Sure. We have to be silent." Mrs. Fitzpatrick placed a finger to her lips. "We can not interrupt them."
" Interrupt that?" "You'll see."

***

After waiting on the 3 ladies to conclude once more, Mrs. Fitzpatrick blazed a trail into the barn. Sidney took a deep breath and also let it out. Her breath hung in a cloud simply in front of her face. Regardless of her handwear covers, her fingers really felt tight from the cool practically quickly. She flexed them, trying to stay cozy, while Mrs. Fitzpatrick dug in the workdesk drawer for a flashlight.
" It wasn't the excellent night for this, yet everything appears okay currently,"

Mrs. Fitzpatrick said. She switched over the flashlight on as well as gave

Mary a wink. "I assume you'll be truly shocked."
The older lady led them to Sadie's stall by the beam, not troubling to turn the barn lights on, and she leaned over the leading fifty percent of the stall door, overlooking.
" What are you looking at?" Mary asked. "Sadie's standing up again!"
Sadie stood with her head hanging, biting tiredly on hay from her manger. She really did not look perspiring or upset any longer, simply exhausted.
Mrs. Fitzpatrick intended the light beam down at Sadie's feet. There, snuggled in the fresh timber shavings on the delay floor, was a little steed. A foal.
Mary screeched, and the baby horse snagged its head up. Mrs. Fitzpatrick placed a finger to her lips once again. "Remember. Quiet. Mother and also infant require to relax."
" But I didn't understand," Mary claimed. "Why didn't I recognize?"
" Your father recognized, as well as he informed me. That's why Sadie needed to have all the special feeds and attention. She required it because she was anticipating a child. Didn't you see that she 'd gotten bigger?"
" I thought she was just getting fat standing in her delay throughout the day," Mary claimed with a laugh. "Where we utilized to live, she had a whole pasture to herself, so I assumed she wasn't getting sufficient exercise. Why would not Daddy want me to know?"
" Your daddy really did not want you to stress over her, as well as he intended to shock you. He knows exactly how special she is to you."
Sidney whistled and drank her head. "This is insane." She hadn't paid much interest to Sadie considering that she was prohibited from caring for the horse, so she had not discovered her growing belly. All the weird policies made a lot more feeling now, though. Expectant mares needed to be on special diets occasionally, and Mary's papa wouldn't have actually wanted any individual to mess that up.
Sidney poked her head over the delay close to Mary, as well as Jane pushed in between them. They aahed as well as oohed over the foal with each other.
" It's a little boy." Mrs. Fitzpatrick gave the flashlight to Mary, that ran the light over the foal's unclear body. His coat was a dark brownish color, and he had a small white celebrity right in the center of his forehead.
" He's beautiful. Mom would certainly've enjoyed him."
Mary choked up a little bit, splits involving her eyes, and Sadie moved over, stepping thoroughly around her brand-new fee, to nuzzle Mary's hand.
" Why didn't you tell me tonight?" Mary asked her riding trainer.

" I thought she was dying."

Mrs. Fitzpatrick trembled her head as well as squeezed her jaw. "Things were looking negative there for a while. She had some troubles. And also one reason you really did not observe just how big she 'd grown is because she wasn't fairly prepared to have him yet. He came early."
" So she remained in difficulty?" Mary asked.
Mrs. Fitzpatrick responded. "Oh, yes. I definitely had not been pretending. As well as you require to say thanks to Dr. Parsons. He did a terrific work with her, and also he's not also your routine veterinarian. He supplied the foal while we were out caroling. Then he stayed to make sure every little thing would be alright with mom and child. He really did not want you to come out and also see her till he recognized they would both be fine."
" Where is Dr. Parsons currently?"
" He went on home to obtain some remainder. The poor man was half-frozen."
Mary ran her pass on Sadie's temple and pleased the hairs on the equine's nose.
" I'll make certain to thank him directly. I nearly lost you tonite, Sadie. However thanks to Dr. Parson, I got an additional equine instead. An additional friend. More than one, in fact." She relied on look at Sidney and also Jane, that grinned back at her.
Sidney shuddered as well as scrubed her gloved hands together. She can hear the wind whipping around the barn outside. The weather condition had not gotten any kind of much better. In fact, it appeared a lot even worse.
" Sadie, your baby came right in the center of a snow storm," Sidney claimed to the equine in a scolding voice. "Probably the most awful time he can've come."
" I'm grateful he came while we're right here, though." Jane smiled down at the foal. He stood up shakily, really shakily, on long, slim legs as well as walked awkwardly to his mom's side. "I've never ever seen a newborn foal before. I didn't recognize they could stand so quickly!"
The ladies giggled, and also enjoyed as the foal started to registered nurse.
" He appears like he's on stilts," Mary said. The foal tottered and virtually dropped, and also the ladies wheezed, however he managed to maintain his balance and also proceeded suckling.
" What are you mosting likely to call him, Mary?" Sidney asked.
Mary saw him quietly momentarily. "I'll have to think about it.
He needs an ideal name. One that fits him."

His brief, fluffy tail shivered wildly, and Sadie transformed her head to push his rump with her nose.

" I believe we ought to let them be currently," Mrs. Fitzpatrick said, examining the pair one last time. "They need to rest, therefore do we."
The women nodded, and they transformed their backs on the sweet scene unwillingly to follow their trainer back down the barn aisle towards the heat of their beds.
" I'll let you in on a little secret," Mrs. Fitzpatrick said at the door of the bunk room. "We're going on an early morning trip tomorrow. We can enjoy the sun increase over the snow."
" I wonder just how much snow there'll be by tomorrow?" Jane asked her, rubbing at the goose bumps on her bare arms. They had thrown out the coats that had actually been tossed on over their jammies. Sidney couldn't wait to climb back under the warm covers in the cozy bunk bed.
" I'm really hoping lots. I can send you all out to play while I cleanse up in below." She looked around the damaged location where the party had been, and at the heaps of dishes in the cooking area sink. All the food had been done away with, yet the smells stuck around. Gingerbread. Cookies. Flavors.
" Smells like Christmas in below," Sidney stated, licking her lips. "Wake me up early. I'll help you tidy up. If I can have the very first assisting of leftovers ...".
Mrs. Fitzpatrick pushed and laughed Sidney carefully toward the bunkroom. "Go to sleep. I'll see you ladies in the early morning.".

Chapter 6

New Beginnings

Even with their enjoyment, the ladies slept quickly that evening. Sidney had actually hardly made it back to her warm bed prior to her eyes started to sag. As soon as her head hit the pillow, she was off to dreamland. She really did not wake up till morning when Mrs. Sinclair leaned right into the bunkroom as well as called out "Good morning, girls!".

Groans and also whispers filled up the bunkroom as the girls stirred in their. beds.

Sidney surrendered to look at Mrs. Sinclair. "Mom, what are you. doing below?".

" I came by to assist Mrs. Fitzpatrick with breakfast." Mrs. Sinclair said. "And with preparation for your early morning tasks. Your mom's here, also," she said to Jane.

Jane climbed below the top bunk, scrubing at her bleary eyes. "Food's on the table." Sidney's mother waited up until every last one of. them had risen prior to herding them out of the bunkroom as well as heading back to the cooking area herself.

She clapped and grinned Mary on the back as she passed her. "I fulfilled the new baby. He's simply stunning. Congratulations.".

" I believe Sadie is the one who should be congratulated." Mary smelled the air and smiled. "Gosh, this is the most effective pajama party I've ever before been to. I've never ever had a lot excellent food.".

Plates filled with pancakes and bacon had actually currently been laid out for the girls, and also Sidney ordered one. All-time low of the paper plate felt warm against her hands. She put a generous helping of maple syrup over the steaming pancakes, dipping a piece of bacon in the mess before popping it into her mouth.

She chewed gladly while Mrs. Abbot poured a glass of milk for her. Jane's mother had actually been placed on beverage duty while Mrs. Sinclair mosted likely to the children' bunkroom to wake them up, also.

Rather than fighting for a seat at one of the craft tables or at the kitchen counter, Sidney and also Jane located a silent edge as well as plunked right down on the flooring. Sidney balanced her plate on her lap as well as swung for Mary to join them.

The ebony-haired girl looked far better than Sidney had actually ever seen her. Her brownish eyes beamed brilliantly, and the smile she bestowed upon her brand-new buddies gave away simply how happy she felt. "I can't wait to head out and also see him once more!".
" Me either!" Jane squealed. "He's so charming.".
Mary smeared butter onto her pancakes with a plastic knife. "I truly appreciate what you men did last night. Sticking up for me.".
" It was absolutely nothing. We understand you didn't do it, Mary," Sidney stated. And it held true. Sidney wasn't sure who had actually taken the rewards and concealed them, however she felt certain Mary had not done it.
Bryan and also Jimmy came as well as took a seat with the ladies. After being gotten up, the boys had actually merged on the food table as well as currently a lot of the offering plates were bare. Mrs. Sinclair was active at the cooking area sink washing filthy recipes, while Mrs. Abbot served the last of the stragglers.
" How's it going?" Bryan claimed sleepily. He took a huge gulp of milk, as well as looked from one lady to the various other. "You look rather pleased.".
The girls traded a deceptive look. "They don't recognize," Sidney claimed. "They didn't reach see last night.".
" Know what?" Jimmy asked. His blonde hair stood out from under his cowboy hat, which looked like it had been smushed onto his head straight out of bed.
" About Mary's brand-new steed," Jane stated, bending Mary. "Tell them." The boys looked expectantly at Mary, who prevented her eyes shyly. "Sadie had a foal last night," she murmured.
" A foal?" Bryan stuck a forkful of food in his mouth and also chewed noisally. "What? I really did not recognize she was mosting likely to have a foal. I wish to see.".
" Close your mouth when you eat, Bryan. Gross." Jane wrinkled her nose at the kid. He stuck a tongue loaded with eaten food out at her in action.
" Bryan!" Sidney gasped. "Disgusting. What is Mary mosting likely to think of. you?".
But Mary simply took a bite as well as laughed of pancake herself. "We'll go. consider him as soon as we consume. Don't stress. It's difficult to offend me.".
Mrs. Fitzpatrick, who had been lacking for morning meal, was available in only a min or two later to recruit her very first team for morning activities.
" We're going riding this morning. We don't have sufficient horses for everybody, so we're mosting likely to enter 2 groups. That would love to remain in the initially group?".
Sidney and also her buddies browsed at one another.

" Let's go together," Sidney stated. "We can be in the initial team. It does not appear like numerous are offering.".
It was true. A number of the riding trainees, currently full as well as still drowsy on pancakes and milk, had actually sprawled out on the flooring with games or had mysteriously gone away right into the bunkrooms again. Sidney suspected that a few may have slid back into bed to continue resting.
The group rose as well as got rid of their garbage, signing up with Mrs. Fitzpatrick by the door. Jared, Jimmy's little brother, also came by, in addition to a couple of various other children his age.
Mrs. Fitzpatrick did a fast head count. "Perfect," she stated. "You men go obtain clothed. I'll satisfy you out in the barn. The steeds are currently tacked up and ready to go.".

***.

Mrs. Fitzpatrick led them out right into the protected sector to place their steeds. Sidney had obtained lucky. Mrs. Fitzpatrick had appointed her to her preferred steed in the stable. She placed an arm and also shuddered around Jasper's unclear neck. His wintertime coat had actually grown out, and he looked twice as furry as he did during the summer season.
Jane rode her common mount, Misty. The gray Arabian mare looked frustrated as well as exhausted at being dragged out of her delay so early in the early morning. Jane stalled, holding Misty by the bridle, as well as Misty decreased her head and half- closed her eyes.
" She's still in sleep mode," Jane stated, agitating the reins. Misty opened her eyes briefly after that closed them again.
" Mount up!" Mrs. Fitzpatrick offered the word, holding her own mount, Jasmine, by the reins while she enjoyed her trainees place. Jasmine was Jasper's sis, as well as she looked very similar to him in everything but dimension.
They both had glossy black layers, white markings on their bodies, as well as long, slightly wavy, hairs and tails. She was a lot smaller than Jasper, though, and also she was the only lesson horse Sidney had never ever ridden since she was for innovative bikers just.
Bryan rode Magic, an anxious chestnut Quarter Horse, and also Jimmy rode his own equine, Charlie, who he boarded at Blue Moon Stables. They both climbed up into the saddle. Sidney anticipated Magic to be his usual restless self, however also he seemed restrained. He stood silently, waiting on the signal to

go, while Bryan changed his stirrups.

Sidney swung up into the saddle. She sat on Jasper and fiddled with the equine's hair while she waited for everybody else to place. The younger students took a bit longer.

When every person was up on their horse and established to go, Mrs. Fitzpatrick installed Jasmine and pushed the horse's sides, steering her toward the entrance. Sidney let out a wheeze when it opened. A deep bed of snow bordered the stables.

She glanced at Jane, excited. "Look at it!".

The students all began chatting simultaneously. "We can make snowmen! We can develop snow fts! We can make snow angels!".

Mrs. Fitzpatrick giggled. "Yes, you can. Once we come back. You can invest the early morning having fun in the snow. I think I even have a sled someplace. Be careful with the equines. We're mosting likely to maintain the ride short and sweet.".

Sidney had actually never ever seen a lot snow in her life, as well as apparently neither had Jasper.

When they tipped as well as exited the sector onto the icy mix for the very first time, the horse looked down at the crispy white things in surprise.

Sidney allowed him to decrease his nose and also sniff the snow.

" Take your time," Mrs. Fitzpatrick stated from the front. "Go gradually as well as allow your steeds figure it out.".

The steed smelled the ground thoroughly, after that he took a huge bite!

"Jasper!" Sidney guffawed. "What are you doing?!?".

The horse let the snow fall from his mouth and also grabbed some much more, after that moved the snow around with his nose, excavating for the yard hidden underneath. Seeming satisfied with his experiment as well as with the reality that the yard was still there, he lifted his head, portions of dirtied snow still falling from his lips, and also proceeded walking. The various other horses dealt with the snow just as oddly. They all wanted to taste it and play with it. Their riders' allow them be curious, making fun of their shenanigans. Being from an area where large amounts of snow are unusual, several of the equines had possibly never seen snow before that morning.

After the steeds had actually become accustomed to strolling on the snowy ground, Mrs. Fitzpatrick stood up a hand. "Okay. Enough of that. Let's go through the field." She had actually currently opened eviction. No horses were out to field today. They were all either being made use of in the trip or snug in the barn.

The morning air felt cold, however stimulating, versus Sidney's skin, and also it smelled fresh and crisp. Sidney took a deep breath. The cold air hurt her lungs, however somehow felt efficient the very same time.

" It's so attractive," she murmured. She hadn't indicated for anyone to hear, but the others responded in agreement.

Not an impact disturbed the excellent area of white covering the pasture, and the soft beds of snow, mounded over tufts of yard occasionally, glinted in the light of the newly increased sunlight, which overflowed the trees, dappling the ground in places with dark shadows.

The equines went through the snow slowly, leaving a path of destruction in the excellent white, like a line drawn with a pen on a blank sheet of paper. They trudged throughout the field and back again, the motorcyclists keeping quiet, delighting in the peaceful morning. No person was out driving. No person was busy outside, cutting lawn, or blowing fallen leaves, or doing farm job. Every person was gathered up in their homes, or maybe even still in their beds. It was a best quiet. The kind of silent that comes only with a deep snow.

***.

After the initial team of motorcyclists returned to the barn, the 2nd team headed out, and Sidney and also her friends mosted likely to check out with Sadie's new infant in her stall.

Mary leaned over the stall door and also rubbed the little brown foal's temple. He jerked his tail happily and also nibbled at her sleeve with toothless periodontals.

Sadie looked a lot more sharp than she had the night previously, as well as she battled with her child for interest.

" Jealous, rather lady?" Mary rubbed her horse's neck and also kissed her gently. "Don't be. You're still my unique steed.".

Sadie enjoyed the attention, nickering to her proprietor and pushing her head over the delay door.

" You're tired of being caged because stall, aren't you?" Sidney connected to touch the mare's soft nose.

The child, mad at being disregarded, nipped at his mommy's shoulder as well as.

pushed his head up toward Mary's hand, which was still resting lightly on his mother's neck. When his mother didn't move out of the way and Mary made no move to reach down to him, he let out a little squeal and kicked out at his mother with a tiny back hoof.

"You're going to be a handful." Bryan chuckled. He reached out to brush a hand over the foal's short mane. He had really warmed up to Mary, and Sidney was glad to see Jimmy smiling down at the foal as well. Sidney had taken a moment to pull the boys aside and tell them what had happened the night before in the girls' bunk room. The boys had been shocked to learn about Mary's mother, and they agreed they didn't think Mary stole the prizes.

"Why would she hide them there and then just let you pick up her pillow?" Bryan had said, shaking his head and running a hand through his shaggy brown hair. "It doesn't make any sense."

Sidney had agreed, but they hadn't had time to discuss the matter further. Mary had returned, and they had gone to the Sadie's stall together.

"So, what's the name going to be?" Jane asked. "You've had all night to think on it."

The foal nudged Bryan's arm with his nose and nickered softly.

"He's so active," Bryan said in amazement. "He's got so much energy!"

"Not that much energy. Look at his little legs. They're shaking." Jane pulled Bryan's arm away. "I think he's tired. But he's too curious to lay down and take a nap."

The foal vied for their attention for a few more minutes then dropped into the wood shavings on the stall floor, curling his long legs under him. Mary looked at the little spitfire. The baby who had been born on an unfortunate, and very cold, night in December.

"He's a Christmas baby, so he has to have a Christmas name."

"How about Nick, after St. Nick?" Jimmy suggested.

"I like that," Mary said. She cocked her head and tried it several times. "Nick. Little Nick. Or Nicky."

"That's cute." Sidney smiled down at the foal. He flicked his ears back and forth and lowered his chin to the ground, closing his eyes.

"I don't think it's quite right, though." Mary frowned. "What do you think of Rudolph? After the reindeer?"

Sidney laughed loudly with delight. "Rudolph. I love it. He does look like a little deer, doesn't he? With his brown fuzzy coat and his little broom tail."

"And there's a sleigh right outside his stall." Bryan gestured toward the unused surprise. "These could be Santa's stables."

"Rudolph," Mary repeated quietly, staring at the sleepy foal. "I'll call him Rudy for short."

"That's just perfect." Sidney put an arm around Mary's shoulder. "I think we should let Rudy get some sleep now."

The foal's bottom lip drooped. He looked warm and comfortable on the stall floor.

"Can horses snore? He looks like he should be snoring." Jane grinned.

"Yep. He looks pretty happy," Bryan backed away from the stall, tip-toeing exaggeratedly. "Let's not wake him up. To stay out of his way, we can go out and play in the snow!"

Mary's face lit up. She put a finger to her lips. "You're right. I want to build a snowman."

"Let's build a snow fort, too," Jane whispered, "or a snow castle!"

"Nah, I want to have a snowball fight," Jimmy said. "I could beat all of you."

"Well, we could build a fort first and use it in the snowball fight," Sidney offered.

Bryan waved all their ideas away with an impatient gesture of his hand. "I've got a better idea. We can do all those things later. First, we should go sledding! I think the sled Mom was talking about is in the house." Everyone in the group of friends grinned. It was something they could all agree on.

"Let's go!"

Chapter 7

The Prize Thief Revealed

The driveway turned out to be perfect for sledding. It sloped gently downhill but flattened out well before it reached the road, so there was no danger of the sledders sliding into traffic. Not that there was any traffic.

"I haven't seen a single car all morning." Sidney stood at the top of the driveway with her hands on her hips, gasping for breath. She had just taken her turn with the sled and dragging it back up the driveway after her ride had been no easy task.

Bryan sat on the long, red sled now, revving himself with his feet so he would get a fast takeoff. He let out a whoop as he pushed off and shot down the hill.

"No one wants to drive in this," Jane agreed. "It's too slick."

Sidney heard a door slam, the door of her own house. Her father stepped out onto the front porch of the Sinclairs' house across the road. She waved and her father waved back, a coffee cup clutched in one of his gloved hands.

"It's going to be easy for us to get home, Jane. How are the other kids' parents going to come get them?" Sidney looked around at the other children, playing in the snow. Several snowmen had been built, a small fort had been constructed, and snow angels decorated the barn lot. Everyone was beginning to look cold and tired. Sidney spotted many red, runny noses and chapped faces. She rubbed at her own nose, and Jane shook her head.

"I don't know but I could use a hot drink," she said. "What do you think, Sid? Mary? Do you want to take a break?"

"Definitely," Mary said. "I need get out of the cold and sit down. It was a long night, and I don't think I've fully recovered."

Sidney agreed gratefully, too. She didn't want to be a party pooper, but she really needed to warm up and rest for a while, and if her mother was coming over she would like to talk to her. She still hadn't figured out why her parents were acting so strange and secretive.

"We're going in," Jane yelled to Bryan, who was trudging back up the hill, pulling the sled by its string. Jimmy was almost halfway down, about to grab the sled for his turn.

"We'll come in, too," Bryan replied, handing the sled off to his friend. "Just one more ride."

Sidney, Jane, and Mary tramped through the snow and back into the barn addition, stopping at the door to remove their boots and snow-covered clothing.

Mrs. Fitzpatrick met them in the entryway. "Hot cider? You three look like you're freezing."

"We are." Sidney unwrapped her scarf and hung it by the door. The girls discarded the rest of the their outerwear in record speed and followed their riding instructor into the kitchen.

Pouring out hot cider, she handed a mug to each girl. "It's really hot. Be careful. You might want to wait a few minutes to drink it."

Sidney gasped at the warmth of the mug in her hands and quickly set it down on the counter. While they waited on the scalding cider to cool, they chatted about the horses, the morning ride, and the snow.

"Well, how's the party been overall?" Mrs. Fitzpatrick asked finally. "Have you enjoyed yourselves?"

The girls nodded, and Sidney picked up her mug to sip the steaming liquid cautiously.

"It's been… exciting," Sidney responded. "I've never been to a party like this one."

"I know I won't forget it," Mary agreed. She blew over the top of her cider, creating ripples in the cinnamon-scented liquid.

"Well, I hope that's an endorsement." Mrs. Fitzpatrick laughed. "Despite everything that happened, I'm planning on doing it again next year."

Mrs. Sinclair came in from outside, shivering as she removed her winter coat. "Mmmm. It smells like Christmas in here. What is that?"

Mrs. Fitzpatrick laughed again. "I think it's a mixture of the hot cider and the Christmas tree I just dragged in."

She gestured toward a small tree leaning against the wall. "It was supposed to be here before the party, but in all the chaos and with the weather, it never got set up."

Jane studied the bare Christmas tree. "It's cute. It could use some decorations, though."

"Your mother went to get decorations from the house," Mrs. Fitzpatrick responded. "She's in charge of fixing it up. You know how good she is at that stuff. We have a little surprise for you guys, and your mom thought we definitely needed a decorated Christmas tree for it."

"There are too many surprises at this party," Sidney complained, but she felt a glimmer of excitement. "I can't keep track of them all."

"Speaking of surprises…" Jane nudged Sidney with her elbow and gave her a look. "Ask her."

The two girls stared at Mrs. Sinclair.

"Ask me what?" Mrs. Sinclair raised an eyebrow.

"I overheard you and Mrs. Fitzpatrick talking last night…" Sidney bit her lip and looked down at the tabletop.

"What did you hear?" Mrs. Sinclair's green eyes widened. "That was a private conversation, Sid."

"I know, Mom," Sidney said. "I'm sorry."

She paused, trying to think of something to say and just as she was about to open her mouth BAM! The door banged open and Derek burst in from outside. Sidney frowned. He had been causing trouble again that morning, picking on the smaller children who were playing in the snow. She didn't want to have to deal with him again.

He slid into the kitchen area on wet, snowy boots. "I know who did it!" He gasped for breath and tore at the scarf around his neck. "I know who did it!"

Mrs. Sinclair stood up quickly, setting her cup down on the counter. "Know who did what? What's wrong?"

"Took the prizes," Derek gasped out. "I've found the person who stole them." He put his hands on his hips and threw his head back triumphantly. "You're never gonna guess."

Mary rolled her eyes and set her cup down as well. "Are you going to accuse me again, Derek? I've already been blamed for it, and I didn't do it. I've already been over this."

Derek snorted derisively. "No, Mary. I don't think you did it. That was Jimmy... and lots of other people."

"What was me?" Jimmy and Bryan walked in behind Derek. "And who left the door open? There's snow getting everywhere."

Bryan closed the door behind them, shutting off the flow of cold air.

"You thought I stole the prizes," Mary said to Jimmy, staring him straight in the face.

"Only at the very beginning. Not… not anymore," Jimmy stuttered.

He removed his coat and gloves, not meeting Mary's gaze. "I don't think you did it. It would be too obvious. If you took them, you wouldn't hide them in your stuff like that. Right on your bed where anyone could find them."

Derek stomped his foot, angry at all the attention being stolen away from him. "Listen up! It wasn't Mary."

They all turned to stare at Derek and he grinned with a mean gleam in his eye. "But I know who it was." He paused, staring at Jimmy.

"Well?" Jimmy threw his hands in the air. "Are you going to tell us?"

Derek opened his mouth, savoring the moment, but before he could get it out, the door creaked open again a little head poked in. "I know what he's going to tell you, and I want to be the one to do it."

The small figure inched into the room, looking from face to face, nervously twisting his hands together in front of him.

"I took the prizes. I hid them in Mary's bed. I'm the thief."

***

"Well, that was a surprising turn of events," Sidney said. Derek had stomped from the room with a scathing glance at Jared, who he blamed for ruining his great revelation, and Mrs. Sinclair and Mrs. Fitzpatrick had marched off with Jared.

"Why would he do that?" Jimmy lowered his brows and slammed a fist onto the kitchen counter. "He's not the kind of kid that would steal."

"Do you really not know, Jimmy?" Jane put a hand on his shoulder. "He did it for you."

"For me?"

"You were so angry and upset when Mary was winning all the games. Don't you see how he looks up to you? How much he admires you? I think he was just trying to help you."

Sidney nodded in agreement. "He wanted to impress you, Jimmy."

Jimmy looked around at his friends. "I'm sorry, guys. I didn't mean to be such a bad loser."

He looked at Mary, who met his gaze with a smile. "I think bad loser is a bit of an understatement," she said. "But I'll forgive you. Maybe we can do a rematch sometime?"

"Yeah, a rematch."

Jimmy put out a hand and Mary took it, shaking it gently. "Friends?"

"Friends." Mary smiled.

"Do you think Jared will be in big trouble with Mrs. Fitzpatrick?" Jimmy asked quietly, hanging his head.

Sidney gave him a quick hug. "No, but maybe you should go explain to her, and to Jared, what happened, and tell Jared that he doesn't need to you impress you. You're already impressed."

"That's true," Jimmy said. "His riding has improved so much over the last couple months. He works really hard at it. Harder than I ever did at his age."

"It's because he wants to be just like you, Jimmy."

"Well, I'll go talk to him, and to Mrs. Fitzpatrick. I'll make sure she knows this is my fault."

Jimmy walked off slowly, looking thoughtful.

"I think this is good for the both of them," Jane said, watching him go. "It'll open his eyes to how much Jared looks up to him. That kid pays attention to everything he does. He needs to be a good role model for him."

Bryan picked up an empty mug and filled it with cider. "Yeah. It annoys him being followed around all the time, though. That's one of the reasons we disappeared at the party last night. He was tired of Jared bugging him. He gets teased for it, you know, when his little brother constantly tags along."

Sidney frowned. "Boys are ridiculous. If I had a little sister, I'd want her to follow me around and look up to me."

"Yeah, right. You hate it when Derek follows you around at the stables," he said, pointing an accusing finger at Sidney.

"That's different."

"No, it isn't." Bryan sipped from his cup and gagged. "This is blazing hot." He set the cup back down on the counter. "Derek bothers you all the time because he's bored and he doesn't get any attention. That's why he's such a troublemaker, too."

Jane stared at Bryan, realization dawning on her face. "I think you're right."

"You don't have to sound so surprised." Bryan looked offended. "I know what I'm talking about."

Sidney crossed her arms and stared at the table, frowning. "I never thought of it that way. I guess I am pretty mean to Derek sometimes when he really just wants to help or talk to me."

Mary stood up. "I think we should all pay attention to people more," she said, "and not take them for granted. I know that better than anyone, and I've been terrible about it. I'm going to try harder from now on, though"

Sidney looked up at her new friend. "You're right, Mary. I'll make more of an effort with Derek."

"And I promise to be nicer," Mary responded. "Not just with Derek, but with everyone. Maybe then I won't be the most hated girl at the stables." A smile tugged at the corners of her mouth. "But I'll still be the best at games. Just wait until we try them on horseback. I'll have you all beat."

"Wanna bet?" Sidney grinned. She always enjoyed a little friendly competition.

***

In the end, Jared didn't get into trouble for taking the prizes. He apologized to everyone, and Mrs. Fitzpatrick proposed that the games continue. And they did, with Mary coming out the clear winner.

When the games had finished, Mrs. Fitzpatrick handed Mary the golden horseshoe and the gift card with a smile. "The horseshoe may not be very useful, but you can use the gift card to buy Rudy a few things."

"Thanks, Mrs. Fitzpatrick, but I'm not going to keep the gift card. The horseshoe is what really matters to me, and I have a feeling there will be some presents under the tree for Rudy. Dad mentioned as much when I talked to him on the phone a little while ago."

She held the horseshoe to her chest, and looked up at her riding instructor with shining eyes. "I'll treasure this forever. It's special."

"Then what are you going to do with the gift card?" Mrs. Fitzpatrick asked, looking pleased.

"I'd like to give it to Sidney."

Sidney stared at her friend, surprised. "What?"

Mary forced the card into her hands. "Just take it, Sid. You were so great last night, calling the vet and waiting with me. And you and Jane both stood up for me and believed me when Penny accused me." She smiled a shy smile. "I want you to have it."

Sidney took the card and held onto it. "Thanks, Mary."

"You deserve it, Sidney. I just wish I had something for all of you." She looked at Jane, Bryan, and Jimmy. "I feel like you're all my friends now."

The little group smiled back at her, and Mrs. Fitzpatrick held up her hand.

"Well, it's time for my final Christmas party surprise. I've just gotten word that some parents are battling their way through the snow to come pick you up." Her eyes roved over the students gathered around her. "I'll have to make this fast."

She turned toward the door and put her hand up beside her mouth. "Santa? Santa Claus?"

"Santa?" Jane giggled, turning to Sidney. "Really?"

"What? You didn't think Santa would make an appearance at a Christmas party?" Mrs. Fitzpatrick replied, and the door opened, revealing a very plump Santa Claus with a huge red satchel thrown over his shoulder.

"Ho! Ho! Ho!" Santa cried, taking long strides into the room. "I've got some presents for you!"

Some of the kids murmured to one another and pointed, and some just stared. No one had expected Santa Claus to show up. The large, bearded man went from one student to the next handing out presents. The packages were all wrapped with different colored Christmas paper and were varying sizes and lengths.

"Who got these presents for us?" Derek asked suspiciously when he was handed his.

"Why I did, of course." Santa laughed a deep, hearty laugh, slapping his knee.

Derek ripped the paper off his gift. "No way!"

"What is it?" Mrs. Fitzpatrick beamed.

"New riding boots! They're in my size, too."

"I got a new helmet!" Another girl cried from across the room.

Santa bent down on one knee in front of Sidney and handed her a gift. The silver wrapping paper glittered in the light. She looked into Santa's eyes. That teasing gleam looked familiar. Could it be?

"Thanks, Santa."

She could see his smile through his white beard. "You're welcome, Sidney Sinclair."

"How did you know my name?" Sidney narrowed her brown eyes and searched the face for clues, but most of it was covered up with a big beard. He also had on glasses, and his fuzzy white and red hat was pulled down low over his forehead.

"I know a lot of things. I know this isn't your last Christmas surprise. You'll have a big one on Christmas morning."

She wanted to ask more, but she saw Mrs. Fitzpatrick watching her, waiting on her to open the gift. Mrs. Fitzpatrick waved a hand at her, gesturing for her to hurry. She looked too excited for Sidney to ignore her, and when Sidney looked back, Santa had moved on to the next child.

Sidney peeled the wrapping paper off her package to reveal a plain white box, the kind that usually holds clothes. She lifted the lid off. Nestled inside was a brand new pair of breeches. "These are kind that professional riders wear," Sidney said in awe.

Mrs. Fitzpatrick sidled over. "Do you like them?"

Sidney lifted them out of the box and held them up. "I love them! I wasn't expecting anything."

"Well, it's been a good year. And I wanted to reward my students for their hard work and dedication. The parents helped out, too."

"Can I go try them on?" Sidney asked. "I can't wait to wear them!"

"Sure, but be careful. You'll need to keep them in good shape for when you start showing this summer." Mrs. Fitzpatrick winked and walked off, leaving Sidney gaping behind her.

"Showing?"

Jane squealed and grabbed Sidney's hand. "Look what I got!" She held out a pretty silver necklace decorated with little horseshoes.

"That's beautiful, Jane."

Squeals and excited yells were going up all the around the room, but all Sidney could hear were Mrs. Fitzpatrick's last words. *When you start showing this summer....*

Chapter 8

The Final Surprise

The party finally ended just after noon when the last parent struggled up the snowy driveway to pick up the last child, which just happened to be Derek, the little troublemaker.

Jimmy and Jared had gone home about an hour before, and Mary's father had arrived only moments after their departure. The party goers had slowly dwindled until only Bryan, Sidney, Jane, and Derek were left.

Sidney walked out with the Derek to meet his mother, and she smiled and waved as the boy climbed into his parent's mini-van.

"See you at lessons next week," Sidney said. "I may need your help with a few things."

Derek beamed back at her and nodded. "Awesome." He slammed the car door and Sidney watched the van crawl carefully back down the driveway, the tires crunching on the snow.

She paused, surveying the messy barnyard. The snow had been disturbed all around the barn. The noon sun had begun to melt the snow, and the snowmen looked a little droopy. A carrot nose had fallen into the snow at Sidney's feet, and she picked it up.

"A carrot for Rudolph," she said to herself quietly, and she went back into the barn.

The horses munched on their hay, content in the comfort of their stalls. Sidney leaned over Sadie's stall door.

"How are you doing, girl?" she asked, rubbing the horse's neck. "Feeling better?"

She stuck the carrot out, holding it flat on her palm, and Sadie picked it up, crunching it loudly with her teeth. Orange juice ran from her mouth and dripped onto the wood shavings on the floor.

Rudy watched with interest, nudging at his mother's chest.

"You can't eat carrots just yet, Buddy." Sidney reached out and touched the foal's fuzzy back. The baby horse flinched and gazed up at her, annoyed.

"You'll like it one day. Look at your mom. She loves to be petted."

The foal flicked his brown ears back and forth then turned his back on her. *Arrogant little thing.* She giggled at the haughty look in his bright brown eyes.

"Well, I better get inside and start cleaning with the rest of them," Sidney said to the horses. Rudy ignored her, but Sadie pointed an ear toward Sidney, listening. *Horses always listen*, Sidney thought, and she pushed away from the stall.

Sidney's and Jane's mothers almost had the party area spic and span again, though, and they didn't need much help.

"You two have been amazing," Mrs. Fitzpatrick said, looking from Mrs. Sinclair to Mrs. Abbot. "I have a little something for you to thank you."

The two women glanced at one another, surprised.

"I think you've given out plenty of gifts already." Mrs. Sinclair laughed. "Even I wasn't expecting Santa Claus."

"Well, just two more." Mrs. Fitzpatrick went to the utility closet and pulled out a box, opening it up. "Shirt size?" She held out an armful of baby blue T-shirts.

Mrs. Sinclair grabbed one and unfolded it. "A small. Perfect. And it's just beautiful." Large black letters spelled out Blue Moon Stables across the front of a shirt, and a full moon hovered just behind the words.

Mrs. Abbot picked out one of the shirts, too, and slipped it over her head right over the top of her Christmas sweater.

"Cool. I want one, Mom," Bryan said. He threw down the rag he had been using to wipe down the tables and dug through the box of T-shirts until he came across one his size.

He discarded his jacket and put the shirt on, modeling it for everyone.

Sashaying down the hallway, he did a small spin at the end then walked back like he was on a catwalk.

Jane snorted, trying to hold her laughter in. "You're ridiculous, Bryan."

Mrs. Fitzpatrick chuckled, too. "The shirts did turn out well, though. In fact, this entire venture has turned out better than I ever could have expected. My dream of owning stables has come true. Not many people can say that, can they? That they're living their dream?"

"No, they can't. And you put on a great party, Mrs. Fitzpatrick," Sidney said, seeing the joy in everyone's eyes. "Everyone had a great time. I think it was success."

“Thank you, Sidney. It was rocky there for a while but the Christmas spirit always comes through in the end, doesn’t it?”

Sidney met her instructor’s glowing eyes and grinned. “Yes, it does.”

***

“Wake up, Sidney!” Sidney’s eyes flew open. The loud knock on her bedroom door repeated. “It’s Christmas morning!”

Sidney sat up groggily. “I’m coming. Don’t start without me!”

“I’ll make the hot chocolate and cinnamon rolls. Get dressed and come down stairs,” her mother said from the other side of the door.

Sidney didn’t respond. She just rolled out of her rumpled bed and staggered to her dresser drawers, pulling out a shirt and a pair of jeans.

“Shower?” Sidney said aloud to herself then shook her head. A shower could wait until later. After presents.

She tugged off her nightgown and replaced it with real clothes, brushed her hair and teeth quickly, and stormed down the stairs. By that time, she had fully awakened, and she could smell the cinnamon rolls baking in the kitchen. Licking her lips, she made her way toward the smell, avoiding looking at the Christmas tree. She wanted to wait until she was ready to rip the presents open to look at the gloriousness of the Christmas tree on Christmas morning. It was always a vision she savored.

Her mother stood in front of the stove, spatula in hand, her ginger-colored hair mussed and unbrushed. Her mother acted more like a child on Christmas morning than Sidney did. She loved to be the first person up, and she usually dragged everyone out of bed earlier than they would’ve liked so they could all open presents. This morning she seemed extra eager.

“Your dad should be down any minute.” Mrs. Sinclair poured out a cup of hot chocolate for her daughter, adding a handful of oversized marshmallows. “Are you excited?” She handed Sidney the warm cup and turned back to the stove, not waiting for an answer. How could anyone not be excited on Christmas morning?

She pulled out the tray of cinnamon rolls and set them out to cool on the cooling rack with the spatula.

“I smell something delicious!” Sidney’s father said, walking in from the living room. He hooked a thumb back toward the tree. “And did you see all those presents? Someone must have been good this year.”

He gave Sidney a swift peck on the cheek as he passed. “Ready to open them up?”

Sidney nodded. “Can we start now?” Excitement bubbled up in her stomach, and she took a small sip of her hot chocolate.

“Sure. Just let me grab one of these delicious cinnamon rolls.” Her father scooped up an un-iced cinnamon roll and popped it into his mouth. “Oh, that’s hot!” He chewed quickly and swallowed.

“Of course it is! It just came out of the oven. I haven’t even put the icing on them yet.” Sidney’s mother put her hands on her hips. “Now it’s your job.” She forced the icing bag into Mr. Sinclair’s hands.

After Mr. Sinclair finished icing the cinnamon rolls, Mrs. Sinclair helped him plate them up and fixed hot chocolates for both of them.

“Now we’re ready,” he said, leading the way into the living room, carefully balancing the plate of cinnamon rolls in one hand while holding his hot cup of cocoa in the other.

Sidney followed, stopping by the sofa to stare at the tree. Multi-colored presents were scattered about under the trees branches. The lights on the tree twinkled and gleamed, reflecting off the shiny wrapping paper on the gifts. Ribbons and bows decorated every package. It looked just perfect. Like it did every year.

Sidney’s father gestured toward the tree. “Dig in.”

Not all the presents were for Sidney, so she sorted out her gifts from the others and handed the other gifts out first. She liked to play Santa.

“From dad, to mom,” she read off, handing the large box to her mother.

Her mother smiled and looked over at Mr. Sinclair affectionately. “Is this what I think it is?”

He shrugged. “You’ll have to open it to find out.”

Mrs. Sinclair tore the wrapping paper off the present and pulled open the box. “It is!” She held up a pretty red dress, one she had been admiring for weeks in the window of a local clothing store.

“It’s beautiful, Mom! You can wear that to the New Year’s Eve party.”

The Mr. and Mrs. Sinclair always attended a New Year’s Eve party at a neighbor’s house while Sidney slept over with Jane. Mrs. Sinclair went over to give her husband a kiss and took a seat beside on him on the couch.

“Now you open one of yours, Sid,” Mrs. Sinclair said, folding the dress back up and placing it carefully back into the box.

Sidney plowed through her presents. She got a lot of horse stuff and some new clothes and books. Her father got a new watch from Mrs. Sinclair. When her parents opened her present to the both of them, she smiled. She had gotten them a framed family photo. Even Herbert, the Sinclairs' hateful cat, was in the photo.

"I think everyone's had a pretty good Christmas," Mr. Sinclair said, stretching out on the couch.

Sidney sat on the floor amid piles of wrapping paper and discarded bows.

"Well, I guess Christmas is over," Mrs. Sinclair said, gathering the empty hot chocolate cups to take to the kitchen.

"Thanks, Mom. Thanks, Dad. I love all my gifts. You're the best!"

Sidney looked around at her Christmas haul with a smile. She couldn't have asked for more. She was a little confused, though. What was her mom talking about with Mrs. Fitzpatrick during their "private conversation"? Which present could have prompted such a strange reaction?

"What's that noise?" Mr. Sinclair cocked his head to the side and put a hand to his ear.

"What noise?" Sidney looked up curiously. "I don't hear anything."

"Listen." Mr. Sinclair held up a finger.

Sidney's parents exchanged secretive glances. "What's going on?"

"Bells?" Sidney knitted her brows together. "I hear bells."

Mr. Sinclair yawned and clambered up off the couch. "Maybe we should go outside and see what it is."

"Maybe," Mrs. Sinclair agreed. She set the cups back down on the side table.

The three walked outside, the bells getting louder all the time.

"No!" Sidney said loudly when she saw it. "I don't believe it. The sleigh!"

Sidney blinked at the sight. It was the sleigh Mrs. Fitzpatrick had rented for the party. And it was coming up the driveway. With Santa Claus driving it! And a horse tied to the back!

The sleigh came to a stop right in front of the Sinclairs' front porch. The family stood gathered on the steps.

"Ho! Ho! Ho!" Santa leapt down, jiggling a large, bumpy belly that looked like it had probably been fashioned from a pillow.

"Mrs. Fitzpatrick?" Sidney laughed. "Is that you?"

Mrs. Fitzpatrick pulled the beard down. "Sorry. I couldn't resist the costume." She crinkled her eyes at Sidney. "Are you surprised?"

"Very. What is this?"

Sidney looked up at her parents. They looked back down at her, excited, and Sidney's father squeezed her shoulder.

"You deserve this, Sid." Her mother gestured toward the horse tied to the back of the sleigh. The horse pricked his ears forward and looked at her curiously with expressive brown eyes.

"This is Arthur. Your new horse." Mrs. Fitzpatrick untied him and led him over to the steps. "Come meet him."

Sidney stood frozen, stock still, staring at the big bay. He was too beautiful to be true. His black mane and tail had been braided with green and red ribbon, and his dark brown coat had been groomed until it shone. Someone had put a lot of work into this horse. "He's mine?"

She looked up at her parents again, and they both nodded.

"You've been so responsible, and you obviously love riding. You've stuck with it, and we want to reward that. Arthur is a great horse. I think you'll get along together wonderfully." Mrs. Sinclair reached out to touch the white star on the bay horse's forehead.

"That's why I couldn't go to the party. I had to go look at Arthur," Mr. Sinclair said to Sidney. "I'm sorry about missing it, but I was afraid they'd sell him if I waited."

"I'm glad you didn't," Sidney said, still in disbelief.

Mrs. Fitzpatrick pushed the lead rope into Sidney's hands. "He's seven years old. He's a Quarter Horse and Arabian mix. That's called a Quarab. He's been shown before, and I think he'll be a great partner for you."

Mrs. Fitzpatrick's words from the party came back to Sidney. *When you start showing this summer.* So this had been the plan.

"I overheard you talking about a surprise at the party. You were talking about Arthur."

Mrs. Sinclair nodded. "I'm just glad you didn't overhear enough to ruin it." She smiled down at her daughter. "You seem a little shocked. Do you like him?"

Sidney closed her eyes for a moment and opened them again, staring at her new horse. "Of course I do. I just feel like I'm dreaming. I think I'm about to wake up."

The adults laughed, and Sidney reached out a hand to rub Arthur's neck.

"I'll have to get to know him. He's a stranger."

"You'll have plenty of time for that. Your parents are boarding him at Blue Moon. You can just walk across the road and ride him anytime you want." Mrs. Fitzpatrick patted Sidney on the shoulder. "In fact, why don't you come ride him this afternoon? I'm sure Bryan would love to go riding with you. You could even invite Jane."

Sidney threw her arms around her riding instructor. "You're the best, Mrs. Fitzpatrick. Thank you, thank you, thank you."

Mrs. Fitzpatrick blushed, but she looked very pleased. Sidney turned to her parents, who beamed at her with shining eyes. "I can't thank you enough." She gave them hugs as well, squeezing them close to her. "You're the best parents in the world."

Finally, she turned to Arthur. She wrapped her arms around his neck and buried her face in his mane. "This has been the best Christmas ever," she whispered to the horse. "I'll take very good care of you. I love you already." Arthur nickered and nudged Sidney's shoulder with his velvety nose.

Mrs. Fitzpatrick turned to Sidney's parents and grinned. "I think we're witnessing the beginning of a beautiful friendship."

www.ingramcontent.com/pod-product-compliance
Lightning Source LLC
LaVergne TN
LVHW041251150826
845673LV00008B/2542
9798758170687